NO FEAR!

The Calling of
Angels

No Fear!

The Calling of
Angels

LARRY CALVIN

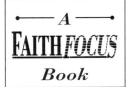

— *A* —
FAITH FOCUS
Book

Sweet Publishing

Fort Worth, Texas

No Fear!
The Calling of Angels

Copyright © 1995 by Larry Calvin
Published by Sweet Publishing
3950 Fossil Creek Blvd., Suite 201
Fort Worth, TX 76137
1-800-531-5220

Scripture quotations, unless otherwise noted, are from the Holy Bible: New International Version. © 1973, 1978, 1984 by the International Bible Society. Used by permission of Zondervan Bible Publishers. Scripture quotations marked TM are from THE MESSAGE. Copyright © 1993. Used by permission of NavPress Publishing Group. Those marked KJV are from the King James Version.

Library of Congress Catalog Number 95-68829

ISBN: 0-8344-0245-9

Printed in the U. S. A.
10 9 8 7 6 5 4 3 2 1

*This book is lovingly dedicated
to my special angel,
my wife, Joan.
Your name means "God's Gracious Gift,"
and for three decades you have been
precisely that to me.*
ILYADYEFI!

Contents

Acknowledgment

Anytime you work with anyone as closely as I have with the Sweet team this year, you grow to feel like family. You're definitely on a first name basis after two books in one calendar year. So, to Dawn, Sara, Patty, Ann, Carolyn, and the entire Faith-Focus team, I say a hearty "Thanks!"

When you produce two books in one year, you occasionally hear comments from your own family like: "Who's that strange man with the laptop sitting in Dad's chair?" So, to my angel, Joan, and our grown children, Jim, Laurie, Ted, and Lisa, I say, "Thanks, gang, for your broad smiles and encouraging words!"

To our new grandson, Caden: If we gave you a penny for each ounce of love we feel for you right now, you could pay off America's national debt and still be the richest person in the whole, wide world. On second thought, forget the pennies. With a mom and dad like yours, you *are* the richest person in the whole, wide world. We love you, Sweet Thing.

My secretary, Maureen Verett, poured an incredible measure of herself into the original manuscript for this volume. "Thanks, Mo!"

The ever-faithful Good News Bible Class gets to be the testing ground for most of my ideas. For their persistence in the face of adversity, I say, "Thanks, family of God!"

I wish I could tell you that an angel appeared to me at the start of this writing and provided me with precisely the words I should pen. It didn't happen, folks!

1

This book is about far more than angels, however. It's about the active involvement of a loving God in the practicalities of our daily lives. In that regard, all who have worked on this project will attest to the fact that His presence has been felt every step of the way.

For that reason I *must* say, "Thanks, Father, for warm bread and gentle whispers. As is the case with everything in our lives, this book could not have happened without You!"

This book is sent out with the prayer that it will help you become more aware of God's powerful presence in each activity of your life. His angels are there! Open your eyes to their joy!

Larry Calvin

No Fear!

Fear is a parasite that saps our strength,
And Satan will certainly pursue any length
To keep us afraid to reach out and grow.
He'll bruise us and batter and bury us so
In a trash heap of worries and turmoil and fears;
His negative power will drive us to tears.

But praise be to God, we can be free.
For the Lord Jesus Christ has caused us to see
That he has not given us a spirit of fear.
For in knowing his word and holding it dear,
We come to know him in an intimate way,
And joy floods our soul at prayer time each day.
And as this love grows and matures down inside us,
We grow in the knowledge that he will provide us
With all that we need—whatever that is.
And he does this simply because we are his.

So, go away, Fear, and leave us alone!
For we know the One by whom we are known.
And never again will you be our master,
To lead us to depression, decay, and disaster.
God is our Father and Christ is our King!
And we love him and trust him for our everything!

Larry Calvin

Introduction

His story was unbelievable. It would have been, that is, if he weren't so personally credible. Seldom in my counseling practice do I see a client so seemingly "together." Enthusiasm radiated from his countenance. His body language spoke of energy, vitality, and hope. An unspoken "Life is an adventure!" seemed to be welling up from within him, and splashing on everyone he met. He was a joy to be around.

Two years earlier, this young man was involved in a horrible automobile accident. Upon impact, his car had burst into flames. Onlookers saw two men appear out of nowhere, approach the burning car, drag this young man to safety, and disappear as quickly as they'd come. To this day, this Christian man and many of the onlookers believe that they witnessed him being delivered from that crash, without a scratch or a burn, by angels from the Lord.

He'd not come to see me for counseling. He'd come for spiritual direction: "Help me discover what the Lord wants me to do. God obviously has a reason for delivering me from that wreck and a purpose for me to accomplish." He found every day exciting as he patiently searched for life's purpose.

I find that kind of pilgrimage a lot among those who believe they've experienced Divine deliverance. Acknowledging God's involvement in our lives seems to change us forever. To use the words I hear so frequently from the delivered, "We're never the same again."

The stories of divine intervention are endless: A

husband is silently contemplating leaving his wife for his mistress when the preacher's words refocus his attention on the wife of his youth. A teenager is thinking suicidal thoughts at the very moment that his dad feels the urgency to tell his son how much he loves him. The boy dismisses his self-destructive thoughts. On and on the stories go.

I think it's time to come out of the closet and announce our belief that God is alive and active in our world today. I share such stories because too long we've blushed to share them. I hope that is about to change.

I use such examples only after a great deal of prayerful pause and concern. Some readers have experienced tragedy, betrayal in relationships, the death of a loved one—maybe even the suicide of a child. You could, at this very moment, feel old, deep wounds of guilt or anger rise to the surface, still lingering from your day of disaster. Maybe you've just come from the funeral of your son who didn't escape his car crash. "Why?" shouts forth from the deepest recesses of your being.

As I write, I am certain that Satan, a fallen angel who disguises himself as an angel of light, does not want us to become too well acquainted with angels, God's agents of intervention, and how they operate. Our ignorance feeds his bliss.

Sometimes we think that disasters could have been diverted if only our discernment had been sharper, our faith stronger, or our prayer life more intense. At such moments, we must remind ourselves that Adam and Eve had the perfect Parent and the ideal environment, yet they made serious blunders and produced a murderous son. Judas spent three years in the best peer group the world has ever known, but he made mistakes and his discouragement over his choices led to his suicide.

If perfectly mature discernment or a strong-enough faith could deliver us from all catastrophe, then Jesus would have turned Judas's life around, and, in the process, could have, hypothetically, avoided the cross. Yet, Jesus' heart of loving obedience to his Father, combined with his love for you and me, could not have allowed him to do anything other than what he did. The Divine Plan must be carried out.

I'll admit to you that this study will probably produce more questions than answers. Maybe that will remind us that our God is a Father of mystery and surprise, bigger than we have ever imagined.

I do know that all of us—alive or dead—are in the hands of a Father whose love for us surpasses our comprehension. He knows the hearts of the hurting marriage partners, the divorcees, and the suicide victims as well as the surviving families of life's many tragedies. His love is deep enough to cover any offense, his forgiveness wide enough to cleanse any soul, his grace great enough to heal any heart, his mercy magnanimous enough to save even me. I can trust a God like that no matter what happens.

So, if the temptation arises to become discouraged by any of these examples, please fight that impulse. Rather, be encouraged by the healing comfort God and his angels are desiring to provide for you right now.

God is alive and active on planet earth! Please allow that assurance to calm your fears, ease your doubts, and ignite your heart with unspeakable joy. He'll change your life for the better—forever. Of that you can be sure. No Fear!

Ephesians 1:15-23

For this reason, ever since I heard about your faith in the Lord Jesus and your love for all the saints, I have not stopped giving thanks for you, remembering you in my prayers. I keep asking that the God of our Lord Jesus Christ, the glorious Father, may give you the Spirit of wisdom and revelation, so that you may know him better. I pray also that the eyes of your heart may be enlightened in order that you may know the hope to which he has called you, the riches of his glorious inheritance in the saints, and his incomparably great power for us who believe. That power is like the working of his mighty strength, which he exerted in Christ when he raised him from the dead and seated him at his right hand in the heavenly realms, far above all rule and authority, power and dominion, and every title that can be given, not only in the present age but also in the one to come. And God placed all things under his feet and appointed him to be head over everything for the church, which is his body, the fullness of him who fills everything in every way.

Chapter 1

From Fear
to Faith

Angels Point Us to the Father

His hands gripped the arms of his chair with viselike intensity. He sat on the edge of his seat. His shoulder-length hair framed his hollow eyes. His paranoia was apparent in his appearance as well as his words.

It seemed the whole world was against him. He'd been unable to find joy anywhere: the end of a needle, the bottom of a bottle, the bed of a stranger. If anything, these experiences had compounded his feelings of rejection, inferiority, and isolation.

The irony was that as he sat in my counseling office, his paranoid stare frozen to the floor, the chest of his T-shirt bore the words **No Fear**. What a contradiction! Here sat as frightened a young man as I'd ever met, bearing the false markings of a courageous hero.

Sometimes we're like that aren't we? A society with more fears, insecurities, worries, and concerns than preceding generations. Yet, No Fear products are selling in unprecedented numbers.

We wear brave faces. We pretend to have it all together. We simulate happiness. But we are afraid. Fearful. At times, terror-stricken.

Gangs. Drive-by shootings. Car jackings. Extremist bombings. With such events occurring across middle America, can anyone blame us for being overcome with fear at times?

As we attempt to cope with such a world gone mad, we turn to Scripture. Repeatedly, we read the comforting words "Fear not!" Often these words are brought by God's special messengers, his angels.

To Elizabeth, the angelic message from God was "No Fear!" To Mary, "No Fear!" To the shepherds, "No Fear!"

The angelic "No Fear!" message is far more than mere words. God is actively, vitally, and dynamically involved in our daily lives. Of that we can be certain. Such assurance becomes, for us, the perfect love that casts out our every fear.

Angels. They baffle us, confuse us, scare us, befuddle us. Yet, at the same time, they intrigue us as few things do.

Angels. They baffle us, confuse us, scare us, befuddle us. Yet, at the same time, they intrigue us as few things do. Our appetites seem insatiable when it comes to learning all we possibly can about these heavenly creatures. Who are they? Where do they dwell? What do they look like? How many are there? The questions go on and on.

More than the questions, though, is the gnawing

yearning within us to know once and for all that we are not alone in the universe—that Someone is there who hears, cares, and understands. Perhaps if angels can be proven to exist, then our faith will be secure. Or so we reason.

Yet, angels can't be contained in a test tube. They do not submit to litmus tests. Understanding angels, after all is said and done, is a matter of the heart.

Few men have so impacted my life and inspired respect from my spirit as has Gene Stallings, head football coach of the University of Alabama. Decades ago as a young youth director, I heard Coach Stallings speak to a packed gathering of teens. His words mesmerized the crowd as he challenged us to become all that God has created us to be.

For years since that day I have avidly followed Coach Stallings's career, first at Texas A & M, then as assistant to Tom Landry for the Dallas Cowboys, as head coach for the Phoenix Cardinals, and, finally, as successor to the Bear Bryant legacy at Alabama.

I fondly recall several visits to Stallings's home church in Dallas during his Cowboy coaching years. His obvious dedication to his family and his Lord shone through the tender way that Stallings patiently hugged his son, Johnny, during those church services.

When someone like Gene Stallings speaks, I listen. So, when I heard that he had shared the following story with family and a few close friends, I asked about his willingness to share it with you. He has graciously agreed. This is his story:

> One night when our son, Johnny, who was born with Down's Syndrome, was small, I heard a noise coming from his room. I immediately went to check on him. When I opened the door, I

discovered not one, but two baby boys sitting in Johnny's crib. They were playing a game known only to them and squealing with laughter. The other baby turned toward me, looked into my eyes with a piercing glance, then suddenly disappeared.

To this day I believe with all my heart that God allowed me to see Johnny's guardian angel momentarily in order to encourage me for the years that lay ahead.

What Gene Stallings is too modest to tell you is that the events of that night made a tremendous impact upon his spiritual pilgrimage and has indirectly blessed the lives of countless others. Many times Gene Stallings has called young couples who've just discovered that their child has Down's Syndrome to encourage them not to lose heart. "Your child has a guardian angel," he'll say, "and don't ever forget that."

God is sovereign. If he chooses to allow me to live my entire life on earth without such an experience, I'll praise him for his wisdom. Yet, I must acknowledge that Paul prays specifically for the Christians at Ephesus that their spiritual eyes might be opened to heavenly realities (Ephesians 1:15-23). If I refuse to follow this clear biblical mandate to seek spiritual wisdom, discernment, and insight, then I must bear the consequences of such a failure to trust and obey.

Angels Everywhere

More and more, people are talking about angels and their presence here. The fascination with angels is evident as I enter a bookstore, browse in a gift shop, or even cruise the grocery aisles. The editor of

TEACH Newsletter well summarizes our nation's current interest in angels:

> Do you believe in angels? According to a recent Gallup poll, half of all Americans, and three-fourths of teenagers, believe in angels. And why shouldn't we? Angels are, after all, documented in the Bible more than three hundred times! And there is no evidence whatever that angels are any less present and active now than then. All that's changed is our frail, sometimes fickle, human belief system. Somewhere along the way we decided it wasn't _logical_ to believe in angels.

> Suddenly, though, in the past few years, we fickle humans have thrown _logic_ to the wind and decided that angels are a good idea again. (I'm sure God is amused.) So everything is coming up angels—books, posters, songs, talk shows, and angel sightings are prolific. The _Publishers Weekly_ bestseller list recently contained seven books with the word _angel_ in the title.

> Why this sudden rustle of angels' wings in America? Could it be that rampant crime and the fear of personal danger makes us turn to the comfort of _guardian_ angels? Could it be that our confusion between the idols of materialism, New Age beliefs, and real holiness beg for a _messenger_ from the true God of heaven to set us straight? Could it be that living in our own self-made hell on earth makes us cry out for a little heavenly companionship?

> Whatever the prompting—whether from the Holy Spirit or from nudgings of evil spirits— angels are back, hopefully to stay and interact in our lives.[1]

Angels at Work Today

What do you believe about the existence of angels
and their interaction in our lives? I believe God is
full of surprises and mystery, and, if he so chooses,
he can and might still do anything he has ever done
and even more. I don't believe he'll do anything that
contradicts his nature as revealed in Scripture or in
the life of his Son, Jesus. But I do believe that he is
fully capable of doing anything and everything in the
world today which is consistent with that first-
century model.

In New Testament times, angel activity was not
only accepted, it was expected. In fact, Jesus taught
the existence, reality, and activity of angels. And, as
Scripture tells us, many in the first-century church
had personal experiences with angels. Then why do
we ignore angel activity today?

Doubts and Detours

One reason might be that we doubt God still
works through angels. Some have fallen into the
trap of limiting God's power as if he stopped engag-
ing in living activity among his people at the end of
the writing of the New Testament. To me that's
heresy. I believe that as surely as God is living
today, he is active in our world. I don't believe he
retired in A.D. 33 or anytime thereafter.

Perhaps we ignore angels because their study
might result in someone's going astray with their
newfound knowledge. This is the same tragic logic
we have used for decades in our stubborn refusal to
preach the gospel of grace. Many have stoically
proclaimed a law message because "we might be led
astray" if we preach too much grace. Abuses will
occur when grace is preached, and God will deal with

such sinful behavior. According to Peter, many first-century Christians were misusing Paul's message of God's grace (2 Peter 3:15, 16). Yet, both Paul and Peter realized a truth we have ignored: we must preach the gospel of the grace of God, precisely because that _is_ the gospel.

> **Angels' primary purpose is to point all eyes and ears to the Lord Jesus and his Father.**

I feel the same about the study of angels. It is not as central an issue as the message of God's grace, but it _is_ a significant element in the development of the Christian's faith, joy, and peace. I believe that to ignore learning about angels because someone might abuse the knowledge is also heresy.

Of course, anytime new ideas are studied, there is a chance that someone will get detoured. Detours take you off course and get your focus off of what is really important. In Scripture, angels' primary purpose is to point all eyes and ears to the Lord Jesus and his Father. If anything else becomes our focus, a horrible mistake will have been made.

In an effort to keep our eyes focused on Jesus, we'll avoid these detours:

1. Creating dogma. We could take our newfound knowledge of angels and try to impose our beliefs upon others as if they must believe it precisely the way we see it or lose their souls. We could also fall into the trap of wanting everyone to be as excited about angels as we are. We must remember that life can go on without our being experts on angels. So let's try to dodge the bullet of dogmatism.

2. *Adopting New Age beliefs.* We could allow Satan, disguised as an angel of light, to deviously ensnare us in one of many heretical traps that exist today. Some New Agers, for example, believe in the indwelling of angels. I'm not talking about angels taking on human form to carry out their tasks, which obviously occurs in Scripture from time to time. I'm talking about a thoroughly nonbiblical belief that anyone can, and should, be indwelt by an angel if he is to become genuinely spiritual. Another New Age trap is that angels bring revelations which stand in contrast to scriptural teachings. We must keep in mind the instruction of Galatians 1 that even if an angel should bring to us any revelation in contradiction to the gospel, that messenger should be anathema—cursed.

3. *Trivializing angels.* This detour puts you on the track of idle speculation—angel trivia. How many angels can dance on the head of a pin? How many angels, in fact, are there? Is there an organizational chart for angels? Where on that chart did Satan stand before his fall? Do all angels have wings or not? The more appropriate question might be, what difference does all of this make? Though this may be interesting information, we must pursue things that can make a difference in our lives rather than satisfy our curiosity.

4. *Seeking the subjective.* Some people might decide to devote themselves to seeking some sort of subjective, goose-pimply experience to validate their Jesus walk. I'm not suggesting anywhere in this book that every Christian needs some sort of "angel experience." Nor am I recommending the active pursuit of such encounters. You'll notice that one characteristic of the stories in this book is that the experiences were not sought. They simply happened.

Because I firmly believe that God's angels continue to work actively in our lives, you'll find me discussing a lot about what they _do_, not what they _did_. I'll also introduce you to many wonderful stories from people I know personally. They are deeply committed to the Word of God. They are not seeking a mystical experience to validate their faith. The events they relate occurred unsolicited and unsought. Those telling the stories are intelligent people of integrity. Most of them resemble the deacon or Sunday school teacher who sits beside you on the pew Sunday morning. As their stories show, they have experienced God's activity in their lives.

My good friend, Bob Beustring, for example, sees God's hand in the events of each day. I thank God for friends like him. Read his story:

> Late one night I was working alone in my studio in Arlington, Texas. As usual, I worked in extremely dim lighting with all the doors locked and deadbolted. In such a setting, it was the only way to ensure safety.
>
> At one point in my work, I sensed someone staring at me from the dimly lit doorway into the front room. I turned quickly to see a man. Fear grabbed me and I thought, "How did he get in here?"
>
> The man said simply, "You're needed outside." With that, he turned and left. I checked to see which outside door I'd left unlocked, but every lock was secure. He couldn't have gotten in through a door.
>
> After much consternation, I decided that I'd better check outside to see what this man meant when he said, "You're needed outside."

Walking out, I noticed a strange car parked at the front of my lot. I heard noises in the bushes beside the car and walked over to find a lady and her son crouched behind the bushes crying. She was as frightened as any adult I've ever seen.

She was lost, had a flat tire, had no spare, and was afraid for her life and the life of her son. I reassured her. Then I removed her tire, got the leak repaired, replaced the tire, and sent her on her way.

The little boy who huddled next to her looked up at me just before they got into the car to leave and said, "Mister, are you an angel?"

I said, "No, I'm just a daddy," but, I *knew* that what they *thought* they'd seen in me, I *had* seen in my shop just moments before.

Are angels alive and working today? Are they pointing me toward the Father? I say yes! And the rest of this book will relate why I believe it. So put on your No Fear shirt, and let's respond to God and his calling of angels.

Notes

[1]Mary Hollingsworth, "The Aura of Angels," *TEACH* Newsletter (winter 1994): 1. Used by permission.

Focusing Your Faith:

1. What does Scripture say about the primary purpose of angels? How does that shape your view of angels?

2. What role does personal faith play in encountering angels?

3. Do you believe that angels are actively among us today? Is it wrong to believe they aren't?

4. How comforting or frightening is the thought of having your _own_ guardian angel?

5. Are biblical teachings on angels reassuring to you? Why?

6. What are your reactions to stories like Gene Stallings's and Bob Beustring's?

7. Pray, asking that God will open your eyes to the angels in your life.

Genesis 3:22-24

And the LORD God said, "The man has now become like one of us, knowing good and evil. He must not be allowed to reach out his hand and take also from the tree of life and eat, and live forever." So the LORD God banished him from the Garden of Eden to work the ground from which he had been taken. After he drove the man out, he placed on the east side of the Garden of Eden cherubim and a flaming sword flashing back and forth to guard the way to the tree of life.

Chapter 2

Spoiling
Satan's Schemes

Angels Surround Us

The letter arrived just in time. I was about to write a letter of my own, and it would not have been pretty. My letter would have had the word *resignation* scrawled across it. I was at the end of my rope. It had been that kind of week. Sixteen-hour days and a seemingly unmanageable counseling caseload had become too much. Lack of progress in several cases was overwhelming me. Prayer was a distant dream, and God seemed far away.

Then came the letter. I'll not bore you with the details, but allow me to share the four words from the letter that jumped off the page at me: "You're making a difference." That's all I needed to see. Suddenly, I was past my pity party and ready to return to tomorrow's clients with new energy and enthusiasm. It's funny how four words can turn things around.

Often such things happen in our lives. Just as

we're on the brink of despair, God steps in and saves us from ourselves.

Deliverance or Discipline?

God's timing is always perfect. Should we expect less? Scripture's first "angel sighting" is a story of such perfect timing—God intervening at just the right time to save man from himself.

We don't need to go many paragraphs into Scripture before we encounter the first angels. Actually, the first "angel" we read about does not appear to be an angel at all. In fact, he once was, but is no longer. When we meet him in Genesis 3, he appears as a serpent. Only later do we discover, especially through the apocalyptic passage in Ezekiel 28 and other biblical references, that this serpent was at one point Lucifer, a "star" in the angel band. We'll discuss him more at length in a later chapter.

One of the characteristics of angels throughout Scripture is their joyful obedience to the will of God. Repeatedly in Scripture, God speaks and instantly the angels joyfully obey. That's important to note here because, for whatever reason, this facet of angel life seemingly gave Lucifer the most trouble. He evidently found no joy in obedience. The results were rebellion and discharge from the heavenly angel ranks.

So, it is not surprising to discover the serpent very early in the human story attempting to rob Adam and Eve of the joy of obedience. He promotes a rebellion similar to the one he unsuccessfully tried to start in heaven.

It's obvious that three extremely important things in God's relationship with humanity are the targets of Satan's seductive schemes: communion, communication, and community. Satan's seductions, combined with human freewill choice, led to the loss of the perfect state of communion, communication, and community which God wanted more than anything for his creation.

Man, by his choice, with assistance from Satan, who was disguised as an "angel of light," rejected paradise. But God would not be foiled. As early as Genesis 3:15 it's obvious that God had in mind another cosmic defeat for Satan. Satan had not been allowed to win in the streets of heaven. Nor could he be allowed to win on planet earth. Momentarily it appeared as though Satan had won. Because of sin, it would appear that way many times throughout the centuries. Yet, appearances are deceiving. As it was in Eden, so it has been in all times since. God is in charge. Things are under control, even when they appear from our perspective to be totally out of control.

> *God is in charge. Things are under control, even when they appear to be totally out of control.*

It is precisely at this point that we encounter our first heavenly messenger. Listen to Genesis 3:22-24:

And the Lord God said, "The man has now become like one of us, knowing good and evil. He must not be allowed to reach out his hand and take also from the tree of life and eat, and live forever." So the Lord God banished him from the Garden of Eden to work the ground from which he had been taken. After he drove the man out, he placed on the east side of the Garden of Eden cherubim and a flaming sword flashing back and forth to guard the way to the tree of life.

For years I thought this expulsion from Eden, angel guards and all, was a disciplinary procedure. When a student rebels at school, for example, he is sometimes expelled—removed from the school as a disciplinary measure.

Several years ago a kindergarten cousin of mine was sent home early one day because she was, in the well-chosen words of the teacher, "having a bit of a bad day." When her grandparents arrived at her home later in the day and inquired as to why she was home from school so early, she replied with a sigh, "Well, I got booted out!"

For a long time, that's what I saw going on in Eden. Then, I took a closer look at the text. Lo and behold, I discovered that the expulsion had more to do with deliverance than discipline. It was an act of protection by a loving Father. God was, in essence, protecting Adam and Eve from themselves. He had not interfered earlier in violation of their freewill choice, but his action became imperative.

A *horrible* thing could have occurred without God's help. Adam and Eve might have eaten from the tree of life and lived forever in the cursed state of pain, tears, thorns, and thistles. God had better things in mind for them. God *always* had better things in mind for them. He was unwilling to sit idly by and allow them to inflict this pain upon themselves. So, he removed them from the Garden, away from the tree of life, and posted an angel guard (cherubim) to make certain that no trespassing would occur.

Later in Scripture, we discover that, at some point, God transplanted the tree, and we will all have a chance to enjoy the tree of life when we get to heaven (Revelation 22). It's interesting that the Hebrew concept of heaven is summed up in the word _Gan Eden_. When we get to heaven—the new Eden— the tree of life will be awaiting our arrival. There we'll be allowed to eat from it and live forever.

Angel Activity

What does all of this say about angel activity— about what angels do and don't do? I see two simple lessons.

Angels do not violate God-given human freewill choice. God did not employ his angels early in this story to prevent the Fall. "Why not?" some would ask. "Wouldn't that have been more loving than to allow such devastating events to occur impacting future generations?"

Consider for a moment the widespread implications of an early angelic intervention in this story. God's early intervention would have, in effect, placed God in the position of making man's choices for him. As a result, we would be little more than pawns on a cosmic chess board. Automatons. Androids. Robots.

While human choice does not account for all suffering throughout history, our choices have created a great deal of the chaos in our world. On the other hand, few things bless our world more than when people make good choices and do loving, unselfish things—not because God makes them do these things, but, to God's glory, because he freed us to choose to do them. Choice is a double-edged sword.

Angels protect us from ourselves. For fear that we take one step too many and damage our lives beyond repair, angels will sometimes step in. As in the Garden, angelic activity often appears to be disciplinary in nature when its heavenly intent is actually deliverance. Because of its disciplinary appearance, some people reject angelic deliverance or fail to recognize it when it occurs. Yet, God, according to poet Francis Thompson, is the "hound of heaven" who exhibits a "love that will not let me go."

Angelic Avenues

In Scripture angels work in a variety of ways. Allow me to identify four biblical avenues through which angels engage in their activity among people.

Human Messengers

First of all, it is important to note that the term *angel* literally means messenger. In that sense, then, there are times when the ordinary people God sends to cross our path become angels when they bring us encouraging or convicting words from God. Two such sentences, spoken at precisely the right times, changed the course of my life. I was on my way out of high school to the University of Texas with a full-tuition drama scholarship when the teacher who secured the scholarship for me said: "God has been so good to you." Simple words. That teacher was certainly no angel in the classic sense of the term, but her words lodged in my heart and ultimately called me to thirty years of ministry.

Years later, during Joan's serious illnesses and our personal faith wrestlings, a surgeon could have taken advantage of our situation if his primary goal had been converting us to his particular religious persuasion. Instead he said, "Bloom where you're planted." Again, simple words, but their impact was profound. Those two individuals *became* God's messengers to me in those specific points in my life when I desperately needed a message.

Freelance editor and noted Christian author, Mary Hollingsworth, had a similar experience:

> When I enrolled in graduate school at Abilene Christian University as a communications major, Dr. Rex Kyker was assigned as my graduate advisor. At the time, I planned to go into radio/TV or public relations. I really had no plans at all to be a writer. During our first and only advisor/ student conference, we were discussing whether I should write a masters thesis or take an additional six-hour course to complete the degree. Just in passing, Dr. Kyker remarked, "You should do the thesis because you're going to be a writer." Then we moved on to other things. Those words, spoken only as an aside, haunted me for years. In 1984 I went to work for a publishing house as an editor. In 1988 I became a freelance author. Now, 55 Christian books later, the impact of those simple words still astounds me. Was Dr. Kyker an angel? For me, yes. He definitely delivered a message to me from God, perhaps without even knowing it himself.

I believe such things happen far more in our lives than we recognize. I recall, for example, one hot summer afternoon on Main Street U.S.A. in Disneyworld. We had just walked into an ice cream shop to get some cool refreshment. In my impatience, I was verbally protesting the inordinate amount of time being taken by the family in front of us. Their slowness stood between me and my ice cream cone, and I was perturbed. Joan looked me right in the eye and said, "I think they've got far more problems than we do." At that precise moment, the dad moved so that I could see their daughter, badly twisted by a crippling disease, sitting in a wheelchair with a huge smile on her face as she took the first licks from her ice cream cone. Conviction pierced my heart. God used Joan's words to awaken me to the selfishness which prompted my impatience.

When my son, Jim, was four, I had just disciplined him for some infraction, when I turned to face Joan's convicting words: "Laurie did it."

Human messengers with divine insights—they're all around us.

I had disciplined a four year old for something he didn't do. He'd known that all along. Now, thanks to Joan, I knew it, too. One of the most difficult things I've ever had to do in my life was to walk back into Jim's room, take him up in my lap, and, with tears in my eyes, say, "Jim, I am so sorry. I shouldn't have punished you. You didn't even do it. I wish I could take it back, but I can't. All I can do is ask you to forgive me. Will you do that?"

He cried and hugged me, assuring me of his forgiveness. We prayed together. His prayer pierced my heart, "God please forgive Daddy, 'cause I do." Human messengers with divine insights—they're all around us.

Heavenly Nudges

In addition to human messengers, God's angels work behind the scenes to provide heavenly nudges which sometimes protect us from ourselves. I know that to be true in my life. I became a Christian at the age of nine. At nineteen, as a Bible student in a Christian college, I became convinced that I needed to renew my commitment to Christ. I almost doubted if I'd really been a Christian at all. In a quiet, private ceremony, my dad took me to the church building and baptized me—again.

In recent years I have become convinced that the Holy Spirit came to live in my heart at my early conversion. Throughout my high school years something prompted me to avoid getting into some of the troubling situations I could have engaged in. I believe that Holy Spirit promptings and angelic nudgings kept me on track.

Some might argue that it was my good upbringing, tender conscience, and my willpower that kept me straight through those adolescent years. I did have excellent parents. Consequently, my conscience is tender. However, my willpower struggles over the years, including my eating habits, have proven that a well-educated willpower is *not* sufficient explanation for my deliverance through the adolescent years unscathed. In retrospect I see several signs of unseen heavenly nudgings, promptings to do this or avoid that. I believe God's angels were busily involved behind the scenes during those years. As in the Garden, the choice was mine. Yet, a protection seemed to be in place to prevent irreparable choices. Why me? I don't know. But, I do know that my thirty years of ministry have grown out of the gratitude in my heart for God's help.

Angelic Form

Angels engage in their protective work in at least two additional ways. Occasionally, they appear in angelic form. Cherubim, for example, are described in Scripture—wings and all (Ezekiel 10). The angels in Eden were cherubim. The angel Gabriel appearing to Elizabeth, Mary, and the shepherds was heavenly in appearance (Luke 1, 2). Michael, the warrior archangel, was a powerful, awesome figure (Revelation 12:7). Not surprisingly, fear is the first reaction they get from those they confront. Nothing effeminate about them. These dazzlers bring pause to the stoutest heart.

Human Form

Somewhat confusing times occur when angels take on a human body (Genesis 19:1). In those instances they do not have the appearance of angels at all, but, rather, the appearance of a person. Whether in Scripture or in life, such encounters are, perhaps, the most difficult to accept of all angel activities. You'll read such stories in this book. Even though these events perplex us, they cannot be ignored.

My friend Aubrey Allred tells his story of a special angel who brought good news to a hurting father.

My friend, Forrest Grubb, and I were eating at a local restaurant several years ago when we were interrupted by the news that Forrest's son had been involved in a motorcycle accident.

Upon arrival at the trauma unit at John Peter Smith Hospital, we learned that Forrest's son, Jim, was not expected to survive. His head injuries were so severe that the doctors suspected that brain death might be imminent.

That news took our breath away, and we walked outside to get some fresh air. Outside the hospital, a large woman approached us, extended her hand toward Forrest and said, "I see your son is in serious condition. I'd like to pray with you."

I assured the lady that we'd appreciate her praying, but that a number of people were already in prayer upstairs, and all that could be done was being done. Feeling protective, I tried to keep us moving, not feeling comfortable around this stranger who had approached us so boldly, but Forrest grabbed my arm to stop me and said, "Aubrey, I'll take all the prayers I can get." With that, he stopped so that we could pray with the woman.

We all three joined hands and the moment was electric. That's the only way to describe it. Forrest and I agreed later that the hair stood up on our arms and necks at the power of this lady's prayer. When the prayer was finished, the lady looked into Forrest's eyes and said, "When you get back upstairs, your son will be fine."

Having thanked her, we turned to walk away. When I turned back momentarily to add another word to her, she had disappeared. The view was expansive, the lady was too large to be a runner, there'd been no car in sight, and where she disappeared to so quickly will continue to be a question in our minds.

When we got back upstairs, the doctor greeted us with a smile and the news that Jim's brain was merely bruised and he would be fine. Now, decades later, Forrest, his healthy son Jim, and I see each other each Sunday at church.

To this day when crises put our church members in the hospital, I find myself walking the sidewalk hoping to see that dear, sweet prayer warrior once again.

It's hard to be afraid with a God who works so

powerfully! Was that lady an angel? In at least one dramatic way she was—she delivered an encouraging message from God. You see, it's God's part to send the messenger; it's our part to *believe* the messenger came from God and give God the glory.

Angels are alive and well! They are here every day protecting us from ourselves and giving us the courage to say No Fear! No matter what.

Focusing Your Faith:

1. Why would Satan be excited that many Bible-believing Christians in America think that Satan is not a living being?

2. Satan is actively working to interrupt your communion, communication, and community with God. In which area does he threaten you most often? What can stop him?

3. Describe a time when Satan succeeded in killing your joy in the Lord. How has God reached out to restore your joy?

4. Do you believe that God's angels periodically protect you from yourself? What have you experienced that makes you believe that?

5. Recall when you prayed for something and, in his wisdom, God protected you by _not_ giving it to you.

6. If you were to meet an angel, which of its angelic forms would change your life the most? Why?

7. Pray that you will receive the angelic help God sends your way during challenging and painful situations.

Genesis 18:1, 2, 10

The LORD appeared to Abraham near the great trees of Mamre while he was sitting at the entrance to his tent in the heat of the day. Abraham looked up and saw three men standing nearby. When he saw them, he hurried from the entrance of his tent to meet them and bowed low to the ground.

Then the LORD said, "I will surely return to you about this time next year, and Sarah your wife will have a son."

Chapter 3

Hand in Hand
with Heaven

Angels Deliver God's Special Messages

The book caught my eye immediately. I don't know why. I'd not heard of its title or author before. Still I felt drawn across the wide aisle of the pharmacy to the rack which held this intriguing volume. Amid dozens of books on various health and nutrition topics was a copy of *Gifted Hands* by Dr. Ben Carson. It seemed out of place. I knew it was important that I purchase this book. It was!

The next few hours were filled with some of the most enjoyable and enriching reading of my life. I couldn't put it down. The next Sunday I was so excited about this new discovery that I talked about its contents throughout Sunday school, encouraging class members to dash to the pharmacy to secure their copies, feeling that certainly such an outstanding book would be restocked by Monday.

What a surprise when I began receiving calls Monday night that the pharmacist was telling everyone that he had no record of any such book ever being sold in his store. I called the pharmacist—a fine Christian businessman—and, sure enough, he said that all computer records and invoices showed no sign of any such book having been on his shelves. He was shocked to see my receipt from his store. He simply didn't know how such a thing had happened.

Several months later a friend at church urged me to secure a copy of Richard Foster's *Celebration of Discipline*. As is so often the case with me, I procrastinated, much to her dismay.

One Friday, while helping my son unload the trunk of his car following one of his frequent trips home from college, I spotted a red and black book back in the corner of his trunk. Retrieving it, I discovered that it was Foster's book. Inside the house, I thanked Jim for picking me up a copy.

"A copy of what?" he said.

"A copy of *Celebration of Discipline*," I answered.

"Celebration of what?" He'd never heard of the book, and had no idea of Frankie's insistence that I buy a copy. No one who had been in Jim's car had ever heard of the book, and no one had access to the trunk of his car. In short, we never figured out how that book got in Jim's car that day.

As I began reading the book, I noticed something else rather peculiar. It was a used book, well-read and marked. Normally, when I read a used book, I wonder why others have marked certain parts, and I proceed to underline the "truly significant" parts of the book for myself. About two chapters into this book I realized that I wasn't underlining anything. The reason: the parts I would have normally underlined were already marked. Someone had beaten me to it. The entire book was that way. Such has never occurred with another book before or since.

I don't know for sure that angels placed those two books for my discovery. Only God knows that. I do know that God is vitally at work in our lives on a daily basis in a myriad of ways that too often go unnoticed. The term *Christian coincidence* is an oxymoron—a contradiction in terms. Everything that happens in our lives—no matter how seemingly small and insignificant—works together with the other events as part of God's great cosmic design for our lives (Romans 8:28). That's good news!

Announcing Good News

You really have to work at *not* sharing good news, don't you. Our daughter Laurie and her husband, Ted, experienced a miscarriage last year. So they didn't want to tell anyone about their subsequent pregnancy until they were absolutely certain that everything was all right. Even though that's a normal reaction, it was difficult because good news begs to be shared. What a relief they felt when their doctor said, "This pregnancy looks great. I think it's time you told the world." They did.

And, if you think they did a good job of telling the world, just imagine what Joan and I have been doing for months at the prospect of being grandparents for the first time. We've just quietly gone about our business, keeping it a secret. If you believe that, I have some oceanfront property in Arizona I'd like to sell you.

So, it's exciting for me to realize that one of the special responsibilities of angels throughout Scripture is to bring a word of good news and encouragement. One of the first such encounters occurs in Genesis 18:1-10.

Hot summer days in the arid desert can get

rather lonely at times. No wonder, then, that
Abraham and Sarah, thrilled by their unexpected
three visitors, prepare a welcome meal. They laugh.
They exchange tales. Little do Abraham and Sarah
understand the pivotal nature of this heavenly
visitation.

The three visitors are on a mission of good news:
"I will surely return to you about this time next year,
and Sarah your wife will have a son" (Genesis 18:10).

What a shock! It's not every day that century-old
people get news like that. Stunned silence settles on
the desert air. Only the sound of Sarah's laughter
pierces the silence. Can you blame her?

What exactly is going on here? *Three* men—God
himself and two angels—arrive with a special message for Abraham. The LORD (notice the all-caps in
the Bible which indicates that the *name* for God is
being employed here) becomes the primary spokes-
person. When the encounter has ended, the LORD
remains behind to allow Abraham to negotiate for
the people of Sodom, while the two angels travel on
to Sodom (Genesis 19:1). These rare moments in
Scripture when God himself seems to momentarily
appear in the form of a person for a specific purpose
are called *theophanies*.

The important point here is that these heavenly
messengers bring good news to Abraham and Sarah.
All their married lives they'd been barren. Now the
news comes of a blessing—they are going to have a
son. The news is incredible. Unbelievable. Even
laughable.

Throughout Scripture much angel activity is
given to sharing this kind of exciting news, such as
in the case of Samson:

A certain man of Zorah, named Manoah, from

the clan of the Danites, had a wife who was sterile and remained childless. The angel of the LORD appeared to her and said, "You are sterile and childless, but you are going to conceive and have a son."

The woman gave birth to a boy and named him Samson (Judges 13:2, 3, 24).

We know the accounts from Luke, almost from memory. Regarding Zechariah, Luke 1:13 says: "But the angel said to him: 'Do not be afraid, Zechariah; your prayer has been heard. Your wife Elizabeth will bear you a son, and you are to give him the name John.' "

And concerning Mary, Luke 1:30 says: "But the angel said to her, 'Do not be afraid, Mary, you have found favor with God. You will be with child and give birth to a son, and you are to give him the name Jesus.' "

Throughout Scripture, angels love to share good news. Fear, surprise, and shock are normally registered on the faces of the human recipients, but the ultimate result is blessing and joy. The good news the angels share is not always concerned with babies about to be born. Often angels bring a word of encouragement.

To Hagar in the wilderness it was, "You're not alone!"—the same message given to others later in Scripture:

To Elijah in a creek bed.

To Daniel in a lions' den.

To Paul prior to a Roman trial.

The cases are almost incalculable where God's angels arrive at precisely the right time with exactly the right words needed in order to carry on. It is ironic, however, that while angels share good news,

they do not possess the capacity to share *the* Good
News with humanity. Angels have no personal
testimony to offer regarding the genuine goodness of
the gospel message. I'm certain that angels could
give a chronology of the scheme of redemption. I'm
equally sure that angels could technically tell a
person *how* to be saved. But, to our knowledge, with
the notable exception of Satan and his demons,
angels have not experienced sin as we have. Nor
have they known the joy of being personally redeemed from sin as we have.

---

*While angels share good news, they
do not possess the capacity to share
the Good News with humanity.*

If the Good News of redemption is to be proclaimed to the world in all its power, *we* must be the
messengers. It's significant that the word *angel*
appears right in the middle of the words ev*angel*ist
and the Greek word for "gospel" (eu*angel*ion). *Every*
Christian is given Christ's great commission and is a
messenger of the *best news* the world will ever hear.

Evangelistic Help

While angels do not have the capacity to share a
personal redemption story, they do become involved
in the process of telling the Good News to the world.
Angels have been eyewitnesses to the heartbreak of
sin. They were present to see the rebellion in the
streets of heaven and to see God's agony over the
selfish choices of Adam and Eve, the people in Noah's
day, and fallen people throughout the centuries.
Angels know, perhaps better than anyone, how

human sin hurts God. They've seen how sin hurts people. They've also witnessed how thrilled God is when a human heart repents. In short, they've seen the blessing that redemption brings to humanity. So it's not unusual to see angels getting involved in the evangelism process:

- Angels notify people of open doors of opportunity for evangelism (Acts 8:26).

- Angels let people know when doors are closed—as happened with Paul on occasion (Acts 16:7).

- Angels bring encouragement to keep teaching (Acts 27:23, 24).

- Angels rejoice when one sinner turns to God in repentance (Luke 15:10).

- Angels also work diligently behind the scenes to prepare hearts and nations for reception of the gospel (Daniel 10:12-14). There's no telling how much angel activity was involved in preparing for the breakthrough in Russia in recent years.

What Can We Do?

What does all of this say to us? How can we do our part?

1. _Live each day anticipating an encouraging word from God._ It will come. We need to be ready for it when it arrives.

2. _Encourage others._ A good word from you might turn someone's life around. We must be willing and actively involved in allowing God to use us and our words in that way.

3. _Be willing to share the Good News._ If the gospel is going to be spread in our corner of the

world, we have to tell others about our personal experience with the Lord. But, we're not in it alone. God's angels are extremely interested in, and deeply involved with our job of spreading the gospel.

4. *Be sensitive to open doors for sharing the Good News.* Be prepared to share. Study the Word. Pray. Learn to personalize the message to your life. Remember angels—theoretically, even Satan, if he were so inclined—could tell the story of Jesus. But no one else can tell your story of what Jesus is doing to eradicate sin and selfishness from your life. You must be willing to be vulnerable enough to do that.

5. *Be sensitive to doors of opportunity that close.* When discouragement comes, we can remind ourselves that when God shuts one door, he'll open another. When someone responds to your Good News, be aware that an enormous celebration will erupt in heaven as a result of that response.

Hand in Hand with Heaven

This is the bottom line: I am a participant, hand in hand with heaven, in the most exciting endeavor known to mankind—the daily sharing of Good News and encouraging words. With that kind of trumpet call each morning, every day becomes an adventure.

I've just completed my annual reading of *Celebration of Discipline*. It has become one of two books in addition to the Bible that I've made it a habit to read once a year. Refreshed. That's the one word to describe how I feel when I've completed this annual journey.

How could I have known what a powerful discovery was awaiting me that day in the trunk of my son's car? Life changing!

And just this week another person shared how he

has been blessed by reading *Gifted Hands*. For years, I've insisted that every fifth grader in America should read this book. I've written book reviews on it and spoken of its contents in speeches to large and small groups.

> *I am a participant, hand in hand with heaven, in the most exciting endeavor known to mankind.*

This week's letter is from a granddad in Texas who, after reading it for himself, bought a copy for each of his grandchildren. A few weeks ago, a letter came from a mother in Florida thanking me profusely for recommending the book. She said that, next to the Bible, her daughters credited an annual reading of Carson's book for the dramatically positive changes in their lives during their preadolescent and adolescent years.

Who'd have thought a simple trip to the pharmacist would have yielded such a goldmine? Unbelievable! A prescription from the Great Physician, no doubt.

God is at work among us! Don't allow anything to blind you to that! In his hand even the smallest discoveries become amazing blessings to countless lives for decades to come. Who can measure his powerful involvement in our lives? His mighty angels are but one way that he intersects our paths from day to day as we travel life's road. He did not retire two thousand years ago. He is among us.

So the next time you feel alone, know that you aren't. The next time you are convinced that no one cares or understands, remember that God does. And the next time you feel compelled to reach out to grab some strength for the journey, grab the strong hand that is extended in your direction.

The next time you feel compelled to reach out to grab some strength for the journey, grab the strong hand that is extended in your direction.

From this day forward be aware that God's deepest desire for you is that you not live another day dominated by fear, but that you respond to his joyous invitation to walk near him—hand in hand with heaven. That's good news!

Suggested Reading

Gifted Hands: The Ben Carson Story by Ben Carson, M.D. with Cecil Murphey (Grand Rapids: Zondervan Publishing House, 1990).

Celebration of Discipline: The Paths to Spiritual Growth by Richard J. Foster (HarperSanFrancisco, 1988).

Focusing Your Faith:

1. Describe an occasion when you received a word of encouragement at precisely the right time.

2. Have you ever felt that an angel opened a door of opportunity for you to encourage someone else in their relationship with the Lord? What happened?

3. How would you explain the difference between your role in sharing the Good News and an angel's?

4. Put yourself in Sarah's place as she overheard the angels' news about her. What would your first reaction have been?

5. What is your favorite scriptural example of angels bringing words of encouragement?

6. If your guardian angel were to speak to you about your greatest fear, what would you expect him to say?

7. Identify your greatest fear. Talk about it with the Lord as if you were talking face to face.

Genesis 19:1, 12, 13

The two angels arrived at Sodom in the evening, and Lot was sitting in the gateway of the city. When he saw them, he got up to meet them and bowed down with his face to the ground.

The two men said to Lot, "Do you have anyone else here—sons-in-law, sons or daughters, or anyone else in the city who belongs to you? Get them out of here, because we are going to destroy this place. The outcry of the LORD against its people is so great that he has sent us to destroy it."

Chapter 4

Hitting It
Head On

Angels Confront Immorality

The picture resulting from Oklahoma City's federal office building bombing continues to become more grim and gruesome. As I write these words, the death toll is near two hundred, with more than twice that many injuries, and the financial cost absolutely staggering. But the numbers are only a small part of the picture. It's the stories that really get to you.

Two little brothers, killed by the blast were buried in the same casket—inseparable in life and in death.

A wife was talking on the phone with her husband at the precise instant the bomb exploded, taking his life.

A widow of two months was in the building for a nine o'clock appointment to get her husband's social security papers filed. The blast occurred at 9:04. She joined her husband in eternity.

A mother needed a social security card for her newborn baby. Their funeral was yesterday.

A thirty-seven-year-old mother of four—a nurse—heard the call for help and answered it. Days later her husband held her in his arms as she died—the victim of a beam that collapsed in the aftermath of the explosion. "Greater love has no one than this, that he lay down his life for his friends."

We reel at the shock of such stories. And we wonder. Who? How? Who would have allowed such anger and bitterness to build up in his spirit to the point of doing such a dastardly deed as the purposeful bombing of innocent people? How could such a thing happen in a "civilized" country? In the heartland of America?

A Moral Crisis

James, the brother of Jesus, insists that individual selfishness lies at the heart of such atrocities. We can hardly argue with that when our recent history seems to confirm it.

> *We've witnessed the disintegration of the American family almost without a whimper.*

America seems to have finally become distressed about the moral erosion among us. The irony lies in what it has taken to bring us to that point. We've sat silently since the sixties and looked on as sexual immorality and homosexuality have criss-crossed our country with unparalleled fervor. We've witnessed the disintegration of the American family almost without a whimper. We've watched as 1.5 million babies per year have been aborted over the past seventeen years—most out of concerns for parental convenience.

Yet, now, gunshots are pounding _our_ homes. Thieves are attacking us in _our_ driveways. _Our_ malls aren't safe anymore. _Our_ kids attend schools where guns are discovered in lockers. Now, we admit, America is suffering from a moral crisis. What it has taken to bring us to that point of admission betrays our self-centeredness.

In the midst of such moral chaos, let's recall one of the most riveting angel stories in Scripture. It's tucked away in Genesis 18:20–19:29.

The two angels who come with the Lord on his visit to Abraham journey down to Sodom to see if the rumors concerning the wickedness of that city are being exaggerated. Upon their departure, Abraham seizes the opportunity to bargain with the Lord concerning Sodom's fate. "Lord, if we can just discover fifty righteous people there, will you spare it?

"Forty-five?

"Forty?

"Thirty?

"Twenty?

"Ten?"

Each time the Lord answers yes.

Little does it matter, though, because as this bargaining session is going on, the angels are quickly discovering that the half has not been told concerning Sodom's evil. The men of the city find themselves tremendously attracted to these two strangers and demand that Lot allow the men to come out and participate in group sex with them. Rapacious lust permeates their souls.

The angels are so repulsed by the insensitivity and inhumanity of the men of Sodom that their announcement concerning the city rings through its streets: "We are going to destroy this place. The outcry to the LORD against its people is so great that he has sent us to destroy it" (Genesis 19:13).

What a powerful story! Three elements converge in this account which intersect at other junctures throughout Scripture and history, but few times more powerfully than here.

God's Love

The first element that shines in this story is the *incredibly* patient love and humility of Jehovah God. Abraham negotiates with the Lord for Sodom. The God of the universe, clothed in a human body, bargains with Abraham. Unbelievable! Awesome!

Why would God stoop to this? Why would he take on flesh? Why would he bother to listen to Abraham's pleadings for a city as wicked as Sodom? Because that's the kind of patient God we serve.

When a cynic attempts to jump to the last part of this story to prove that God is an old ogre who thrills at destroying humanity, I must bring him back to the first part of this story. God loves Abraham so much, and his patient hope that people will repent of their wickedness is so great, that he is willing to engage in an unbelievable bargaining session with humanity.

It is this aspect of God's character that Paul says to the Corinthians causes a stumbling block in the minds of those who perceive themselves to be intellectuals. "Our gods don't do things like that." But Jehovah God does. The incredibly patient love of God is one of the most powerful messages in the Sodom story.

Man's Sin

God's love is not the only message found here.

The second element to intersect the story is the depth of degradation to which mankind can sink. Few other stories so vividly illustrate this as the Sodom story does. The two _men_ of chapter eighteen are identified in 19:1 as "two angels." The story of what happens to these heavenly visitors is not a pleasant tale.

Initially, their desire is to sleep in the town square. Lot knows that's out of the question. He insists that they stay at his house. (The streets of Sodom were about as safe at night as the streets of New York City or Los Angeles or Washington, D.C., are today.)

Locked securely behind closed doors, the angels are still not safe. Driven by lust, the men of the city surround the house and demand that the angels be released to them for sexual purposes. The angels strike the men of Sodom blind and instruct Lot to prepare for evacuation.

In bold contrast to the patient love of Jehovah God stands the incredible self-centered, militant, angry, lustful, immoral behavior of humanity.

Can you believe it? In bold contrast to the patient love of Jehovah God stands the incredible self-centered, militant, angry, lustful, immoral behavior of humanity. Ezekiel 16:49, 50 provides us with interesting insight into Sodom's problem: "Now this was the sin of your sister Sodom: She and her daughters were arrogant, overfed and unconcerned; they did not help the poor and needy. They were haughty and did detestable things before me."

Sodom epitomizes self-centeredness gone to seed.

God's Discipline

Throughout Scripture God uses angels to confront humanity at the point of moral lapse. He does not tolerate evil. That's the third element that intersects this passage. God is patient. He is kind. But he does not rejoice with evil, and he will not sit idly by and be mocked by mankind. We've all seen parents who, in the name of loving their children, have been so lax and permissive that they've produced children with a cynical, mocking, sneering, condescending, self-centered disdain for all authority. These parents have not done their children any favors. They've certainly not done themselves any favors. And society will pay a high price over the lifetime of these children for the parents' permissive approach.

God sends his angels to discipline humanity when his heart is broken by man's inhumanity to men. To fail to do so would ultimately do terrible injustice to the criminals, the victims, and a just and holy God.

The angels declared they would "destroy this place." And they did. This, by no means, is the only place in Scripture where the heavenlies confront humanity and deal decisively with human immorality. Throughout their sordid history, the children of Israel required several such disciplinary proceedings: their wilderness-wanderings orgies, the "every man doing what is right in his own eyes" philosophy which permeates the Book of Judges—the stories are numerous. The words of the writer of Hebrews ring true: "If the old message delivered by the angels was valid and nobody got away with anything, do you think we can risk neglecting this latest message, this magnificent salvation?" (Hebrews 2:2, TM).

God's Love Wins!

Perhaps nowhere in Scripture or history have these three elements—God's incredibly patient love, man's seemingly incurable lust, and God's decisive discipline—collided with such intensity as on Golgotha's hillside on that dark Friday. The unique element in this event is God's decision to take all of the punishment due humanity and place it upon the shoulders of his only Son.

When God's love confronts human sinfulness, *God wins.* And when human hearts respond to God's love, *we win.*

As we observe the angels boldly confronting Sodom's immorality, it strengthens our resolve to do what's right. Motivated by God's love, we must come to the point where we can recognize and respond decisively when confronted with evil. Our family learned that lesson well two decades ago.

When God's love confronts human sinfulness, **God wins.** *And when human hearts respond to God's love,* **we win.**

In early 1974, Joan and I went to our obstetrician because we thought we were getting signs that we were expecting a third child. Our doctor, having just played a major role in the *Roe vs. Wade* controversy of 1973, informed us that with the global overpopulation rate soaring, no couple needed more than two children. So he offered to arrange things for us with an abortionist.

We didn't need to stop and consider that. When you're confronted by a suggestion that is so blatantly evil at the core, you respond appropriately. In such cases, you don't pray—you obey!

God led us to a new doctor, blessed us with a precious baby daughter, and we praised him for his help. Lisa turns twenty-one in a few months—a beautiful (from the inside out), godly young lady. We shudder to think of the joy we would have missed if we'd thoughtlessly accepted the immoral "medical" advice offered us that day in 1974.

As human history since Christ's time attests, mankind may still choose an immoral course. We may still choose to mock the divine. The difference is that now God has given us his *all* to prove to us once and for all that he loves us. If the cross cannot magnetize our hearts, then heaven and earth will someday bear witness that our stubborn refusal deserves whatever punishment God chooses to dispense.

Focusing Your Faith:

1. Do you spend more time being concerned about your own immorality or the immorality of others? Why?

2. Recall a time when you were stopped "dead in your tracks" with the realization that you were about to do something contrary to God's teachings.

3. Have you ever attributed that realization to the act of angels protecting you from sin? Why?

4. When has God seemed to be excessively patient with your sins?

5. Share an experience in which you were disciplined by God and now see the positive benefits of it.

6. How does it make you feel to know that God may be using you as his voice in disciplining someone you love?

7. Pray that your Father will send his special angels to help you confront the most heartbreaking sin affecting you or someone you love.

Numbers 22:31-34

Then the LORD opened Balaam's eyes, and he saw the angel of the LORD standing in the road with his sword drawn. So he bowed low and fell facedown.

The angel of the LORD asked him, "Why have you beaten your donkey these three times? I have come here to oppose you because your path is a reckless one before me. The donkey saw me and turned away from me these three times. If she had not turned away, I would certainly have killed you by now, but I would have spared her."

Balaam said to the angel of the LORD, "I have sinned. I did not realize you were standing in the road to oppose me. Now if you are displeased, I will go back."

Chapter 5

A Donkey's Tale

Angels Appear to Discerning Hearts

Jan Patterson, daughter of our senior minister Jon Jones, tells the story of the time when she took her then-small daughter Jessica into a public restroom. It was the nastiest place Jan had ever seen in her life. In fact, she had serious reservations about allowing Jessica to use these facilities.

The need was pressing, however, so Jan got on with the business of making the restroom visit as safe as possible. In the midst of the proceedings, Jessica looked up at her mom and beamed, "Mom, this is the most beautiful bathroom I've ever seen!"

Curious as to how she may have failed as a mom for her young daughter to perceive this filthy place as beautiful, Jan asked, "Jessica, honey, what exactly is it about this restroom that is so wonderful?"

"The music is so pretty!" Jessica replied.

For the first time, Jan stopped long enough to realize that, indeed, beautiful music was being piped into the dingy restroom from overhead speakers. The music had been there all along; Jan had just been too preoccupied with more pressing matters to hear it. But Jessica had heard.

Isn't that the way it is in our spiritual walks at times? Heavenly strains and celestial chords are resounding all around us, yet we miss their vibrant melody because we are so caught up in things which seem so much more important.

An Atmosphere of Greed

Eugene Peterson's *The Message* paraphrases Jesus, concerning the third type of soil in his parable, saying "And the seed that fell in the weeds—well, these are the ones who hear, but then the seed is crowded out and nothing comes of it as they go about their lives worrying about tomorrow, making money and having fun" (Luke 8:14).

> *Getting ahead puts us behind.*
> *Catching up drags us down. Staying*
> *on top plunges us to the bottom.*
> *And God's voice goes unheard.*

Getting ahead puts us behind. Catching up drags us down. Staying on top plunges us to the bottom. The urgent crowds out the important. And God's voice goes unheard. Perhaps we need to develop the heart (and ears) of a child!

Few would deny that greed dots the landscape of America. Many feel that greed has driven the cost of medical care in this country to epidemic proportions. Corruption, caused by greed, has crippled our welfare system to the point where pockets are lined, not stomachs filled. Greed has prompted such a rash of lawsuits that a massive paranoia permeates the marketplace. People are afraid to say a simple "Good morning, how are you?" for fear that friendliness might be misinterpreted as a sexual come-on. Day-care workers fear hugging a child, afraid that the hug might be misinterpreted as molestation. Our greed has corrupted us, seduced us, trapped us, paralyzed us, and is on its way to destroying us.

Keeping Us on Track

God cares deeply about our ethical choices in such a world, and his angels are personally involved in helping us stay on an appropriate ethical track. We desperately need to develop heart-of-a-child sensitivity to God's attempts to rescue us from the greed that threatens to destroy us!

An Old Testament angel story that emphasizes this point is found in Numbers 22. A prophet of God named Balaam is approached by messengers from Moab, who attempt to persuade him to come curse the Israelites as a favor to Balak, their king. God's answer to Balaam's prayer session is explicit: "Do not go with them." Case closed? Well, not quite.

King Balak is the kind of guy who won't take No! for an answer. He sends his "big guns" the second time, important men with extravagant promises of gifts and honor that await Balaam if he'll agree to go with them.

Balaam goes. His prayer session is a mere formality. He's already made up his mind. The text makes it clear that God opposes his going, and he sends his angel to stand in Balaam's way as a last warning against this venture.

Yet, Balaam is so blinded by his passion for the

prizes awaiting him at the journey's end that he is oblivious to the angel's presence in the middle of the road. Even Balaam's donkey sees spiritual reality more readily than this man of God.

After suffering a temper tantrum, a crippling fall, and a two-way conversation between animal and owner, Balaam plods along on his way to certain destruction.

Lessons from Balaam

This story teaches us a great deal about our God, ourselves, and the interaction between heaven and earth.

God sometimes allows what he does not approve. God did not want Balaam to go to Balak. He made that perfectly clear to Balaam during the first prayer session. Even though God does not give up on a person, he does, at times, give the person up to his own selfish choices.

God keeps after us even when we make wrong choices. That's precisely where the angel enters Balaam's story: "But God was very angry when he went, and the angel of the LORD stood in the road to oppose him." The angel later says to Balaam, "I have come here to oppose you because your path is a reckless one before me" (Numbers 22:22, 32).

Yet, God will not force his will upon a person. God tells Balaam no in prayer, and then sends an angel to oppose his journey. But because Balaam is still bent on going, God stands in his way no longer. He gives him one last warning and turns him loose.

God won't beat down the door of our hearts with a battering ram. He'll merely stand at the door and knock. We must hear the knock and open the door. I think Holman Hunt's portrait of Christ knocking on the door of the human heart best illustrates God's position. In Hunt's painting the heart has no external knob on the door. It can only be opened from the inside.

The minute Balaam realized what Balak was asking him to do—curse the people of God—the matter should have been brought to a swift end. A good, firm, unshakable No! would have done the trick. Instead, Balaam decides to pray some more.

God will not beat down the door
of our hearts with a battering ram.
He will merely stand at
the door and knock.

As children of God, we must know when to say No! to obvious evil. We don't need to stop and pray again—we just need to obey. Balaam, too, could have profited from doing exactly that.

Balaam's story also teaches us a great deal about ourselves and greed.

Greed perverts our judgment. It appears that Balak's second offer, "I will reward you handsomely and do whatever you say," is what carries the day (Numbers 22:17). Notice that Balaam does go back to God to seek permission once again. That seems noble.

Yet, if you track Balaam's story from this point on, it appears obvious that Balaam really wants to go with Balak's men. He merely seeks divine approval for a selfish course of action. All it takes is a hint from God (God is obviously still against it when Balaam thinks he has permission), and Balaam is traveling down Selfishness Highway.

Greed is our first step toward worse things. Tracking Balaam's story from this point on does not paint a pleasant picture. Balaam literally becomes the scriptural epitome of greed, selfishness, lust, and immorality. He models all that we are *not* to be. He personifies evil. And it all starts with greed.

Don't we see that quite often in our world? A man's greed prompts long hours at the office. During those late evenings, he emotionally bonds with the secretary. The two end up in an illicit affair. Guilt over the affair leads the man to drink to escape the pain. Then, he wakes up one day to the realization that he's lost his wife, his children, his business, his wealth, his health, his integrity, his lover, and has come close to losing his life. And it all begins with greed.

Greed blinds us to spiritual realities. This is the most significant message we can mine as a nugget of gold hidden away in this account. Balaam doesn't have the discernment of a donkey! Balaam's greedy desire to see what riches lie at the end of the Balak rainbow closes his eyes completely to the presence of the angel blocking his path. His donkey sees more clearly than he does. Can you believe it? This story would be absolutely hilarious if its message weren't so serious.

The donkey sees the angel and darts right. Balaam beats the animal. The donkey sees the angel and darts left, against a wall, crushing Balaam's foot. Again, Balaam beats his donkey.

Balaam carries on a conversation with a donkey. And he's worried about having looked foolish? The donkey talks back—and makes sense, saying, in essence: "You've ridden me for years, Balaam, have I *ever* done anything like this to you before?"

A startled Balaam can only muster a shocked and dismayed one-word answer: "No." Then, the text says, "Then the LORD opened Balaam's eyes, and he saw the angel of the LORD standing in the road with his sword drawn" (Numbers 22:31). Finally, Balaam sees what his donkey has seen for miles. The donkey has saved Balaam's life. The angel explains: "If she had not turned away, I would certainly have killed you by now, but I would have spared her" (v. 33). Balaam learns at the feet of a donkey a significant lesson on discernment.

How in the world could a prophet of God allow his discernment to sink to such depths that he doesn't have the spiritual vision of a donkey? Discernment, you see, is the capacity to comprehend spiritual truth—to see with our spiritual eyes and hear with our spiritual ears. Discernment is the ability to recognize a spiritual insight when it comes along. It involves having our spiritual antennae extended so that we are prepared to hear a word from God. Discernment is a gift of the Holy Spirit which can be nurtured and nourished by focused Scripture study, prayer (both the talking and listening variety), and spiritual disciplines of meditation and contemplation, worship and witness.

---

*Discernment is the ability
to recognize a spiritual insight
when it comes along.*

God wants us to hear his voice when he speaks. He wants us to respond to the direction he offers. It's not necessarily audible communication; I'm talking about the strong impressions, the gentle nudgings, the closed doors of opportunities. I mean the million and one ways that God attempts to get our attention in order to give some direction to our lives. If, for some reason, we are deaf to such leadings, we will not recognize such an event when it occurs.

Such was the case with Balaam. Based upon the subsequent events in Balaam's life, I believe that Balaam's greed got in the way of his ability to perceive the Lord's warnings. He wanted what he wanted so badly that he wasn't open to any suggestions to the contrary. Even if the message were being brought by a sword-carrying angel.

Aren't we all that way sometimes? See if you recognize any of these people:

- The corporate executive, working sixteen-hour days, refuses to heed his body's early warning signs.

- The mom is moving too fast to notice the gentle nudgings to sit down and talk with her teenage daughter.

- The husband refuses to listen to his wife's pleadings that he and his secretary are getting too close.

- The fiancée rejects her strong feelings to break off the engagement.

- The husband/father walks out on his family for another woman and refuses all calls from Christian friends.

- The teenager rejects his parents' advice as being old-fashioned.

We want what we want. And we want it now. We travel on a treadmill going ninety miles an hour. We're too busy. Too involved. Too overscheduled. Tyrannized by the urgent and ruled by the routine, we haven't the time to "be still, and know that I am God" (Psalm 46:10). What a tragedy!

God doesn't give up on us. He calls his angels who corner us. He uses the donkeys of our lives to try to wake us up. He pinned Balaam against a wall. He got Elijah alone in a cave. He mesmerized Moses with a burning bush in the desert. He isolated Samson in a prison.

He does the same today. For some people, the point of listening to God's voice comes in a hospital bed. To others, it comes in the funeral home beside the casket of a family member. To still others, it is in the unemployment line, or the divorce lawyer's office, or the scene of a fatal car crash.

The tragedy, however, is that so many of us seem to insist on getting completely lost before we extend our spiritual antennae. The Balaam story indicates that such need not be the case. Had Balaam really heard the depth of concern in the Lord's initial no, he wouldn't have come begging to God the second time. But the handsome reward simply looked too good to turn down. So Balaam pursued until he got what he wanted. Then, he didn't want what he got.

Many of us seem to insist on
getting completely lost before
we extend our spiritual antennae.

What does all of this say to us about God, his angels, and the interrelationship between heaven and earth? Its message seems simple: We, as Christians, need to sharpen our spiritual sensibilities to be ready to respond appropriately when angelic heavenly nudgings arrive. In addition, we need to intensify our discernment of road hazards on our spiritual journey, such as greed and selfishness, and allow the Lord to remove those roadblocks from our lives.

We can and should walk without fear when we open our eyes and ears to God's angels. They'll take us by the hand and skillfully guide us to safety.

A friend shared the following story with me after class one Sunday morning. Because of the nature of the details of this story, I'm withholding her name.

> For years my family and I had always gone to Corpus Christi for our annual vacation. It was a given. It didn't even require discussion.
>
> Several years ago, however, I became deeply concerned about that year's trip. Something seemed to be telling me that we should change our plans. I can't explain it. It was not a voice. Just a strong impression that we should not go to Corpus Christi that year.
>
> The feeling persisted so strongly that my husband suggested we go elsewhere. "We need to see other parts of the country anyway." Our trip was interrupted with the news that a multiple murder-suicide had occurred in Corpus Christi—at the home where we would've been staying, had we gone. The woman of the house had killed everybody in the house and taken her own life.
>
> Had our plans not been changed, we would have been lying in one of those beds in that home that night. People can mock and ridicule the idea of strong impressions and "nudges" all they want. My husband and I both believe that we owe our lives to an angelic nudge.

If you think the days of donkeys playing a part in God's design have long since ended, you'll be interested in this story from my friend Trey Davis:

It was dark, rainy, and messy as we made our
way through the mountains of Mexico on our way
to join our fellow Christians at the mission point
which we had frequented in recent years. I had
waited behind at the McAllen airport for three
high school students whose joining us had been
delayed. So it was the four of us on this particular leg of the trip.

After having seen a large truck plunge off the
treacherous, slippery hillside in the darkness, we
found ourselves fighting fear, praying a lot, and
wondering if, in fact, we were even on the right
road. It's easy to second guess yourself in such
circumstances.

The slopes were so slippery that we were pre-
sented with a real dilemma. To slow down or stop
might prevent us from being able to get going
again, but to go on could lead to greater dangers.

I recalled from past visits that one of the most
obvious signs that we were at least in the right
general area was the presence of donkeys—the
primary means of transportation in this out-of-
the-way, poverty-stricken village. I began to pray
for a donkey.

Upon sighting our first donkeys, I assured the
students that we were on the right road. When
they inquired as to how I could be so sure, they
were a bit less than enthusiastic about my explanation. Donkeys didn't seem like a comfortable
place to put your trust on a night like this.

As we talked, however, about the Balaam story,
their confidence grew. In fact, after several hours
of treacherous driving I heard the student in the
front seat say aloud, "Lord, we want you to keep

us safe. We're going to go on, but if we are in any danger, please put a donkey in the road! Don't let him move, and we'll stop right there." I was impressed.

After what seemed like an eternity, we crested a hill and spotted two donkeys in the middle of the road in front of us. "Well, Lord is this it? Will they move? Or do we stop?"

As we approached, our questions were answered. Frightened by our headlights, the donkeys ran. And led us *directly* to our destination. We all thanked God for donkeys.

I believe God answers prayer. Balaam's donkey saved his life, and that night donkeys did the same for us. Our God led us through the storm, kept us safe, and guided us to our destination. The road was rocky, slippery, and rough, but God proved himself over and over to us all along the way. And he did it through, of all things, donkeys.

Focusing Your Faith:

1. Do you believe God still speaks to his people today? What means might he use?

2. Balaam was guilty of not listening to God. How could you be guilty of the same sin?

3. When does greed open the door to selfishness, lust, or immorality in your life?

4. What are you presently doing to nurture and develop your spiritual discernment? How are you seeking God's help?

5. Share a life experience in which you felt blessed with spiritual discernment.

6. Do you find it difficult to be silent and listen while praying?

7. Pray about a specific personal need. As you continue in prayerful meditation, ask God to help you wait in silence for you to receive his response.

2 Kings 6:15-17

When the servant of the man of God got up and went out early the next morning, an army with horses and chariots had surrounded the city. "Oh, my lord, what shall we do?" the servant asked.

"Don't be afraid," the prophet answered. "Those who are with us are more than those who are with them."

And Elisha prayed, "O LORD, open his eyes so he may see." Then the LORD opened the servant's eyes, and he looked and saw the hills full of horses and chariots of fire all around Elisha.

Chapter 6

Fire
and Whispers

Angels Comfort and Protect Us

One thousand two hundred sixty days in captivity. That's a long time. One POW in that Japanese prison in Java during World War II was known to his captors as Lieutenant William R. Slone.

To us in our church, this eighty-two-year-old wonder is known as Brother Reuben, one of the most dearly loved men in our fellowship. What a story he tells of how his time as a POW proved to him beyond doubt the active involvement of God's angels in our lives:

> The Japanese corporal of the guard accused me of espionage because I used a flashlight to see my way in the dark night. They took me before a council composed of a Japanese lieutenant, a civilian, and two Javanese who served as my interpreters.
>
> My hands were cuffed behind me, my feet were

hobbled, and I was shoved to the floor in front of the panel. The interpreter pushed a Japanese document toward me and demanded I sign it. When I refused, the lieutenant began beating me with a club the size of a softball bat. Every time I refused to sign the document, I was beaten. This continued for five hours until the lieutenant turned me over to a policeman who took me to the police station about a mile away.

The Javanese police sergeant was kind to me, and I spent a day and night praying and being comforted by the Lord's loving presence. I did not pray for freedom, because I knew I was to die (in Japan you were guilty until found innocent). I prayed that the Lord would give me the courage to die like a Christian, cleanse my heart of hate for the Japanese, and let the panel see the Lord reflected in my attitude.

The next day, I was again taken to interrogation. This time the interpreter and I were standing outside the interrogation room and the lieutenant repeatedly passed by us in his preparations. I could hear rumbling sounds from inside, and I deduced that they were preparing tortuous methods of forcing me to sign a confession. When the lieutenant passed the third time, I prayed aloud, "I hope God forgives you for this." He stopped, and after my prayer was translated, he walked a few steps with his head bowed, turned and stared at me for several seconds then went inside.

I heard the rumbling sounds again, and he ordered us to enter. Marks on the floor showed something heavy had been moved. I stood before the council, and the lieutenant looked at me and said, "You are an officer and a gentleman as I am. I am sorry I beat you, but that is the method we Japanese use to get to the truth. I think you are innocent."

My whole body shook with emotion, and I knelt before the table so I wouldn't fall. God touched the lieutenant's heart that day. God and his angels helped me feel safe in the arms of Jesus.[1]

Faith like that is hard to find. It was rare in Jesus' day and is hardly encouraged by today's fast-paced Hollywood lifestyle. Several years ago, in fact, the Hollywood power establishment was set on its ear. The winner of the Academy Award for Best Picture was announced, and the city went reeling with aftershock. *Chariots of Fire*, a relatively low-budget British film, to the surprise of most of Hollywood, won the honor.

The shocking thing about this victory is that the film was almost evangelistic in its thrust. It concerned a young man on the British Olympic team who refused to run on Sunday because of his religious conviction. The often-quoted theme of the movie was Isaiah 40:31: "But those who hope in the LORD will renew their strength. They will soar on wings like eagles; they will run and not grow weary, they will walk and not be faint."

The title of the film, however, refers to one of the most powerful stories of angel activity to be found in Scripture—the story of Elijah and Elisha.

Angels to the Rescue

The angelic and the miraculous are commonplace in the life of Elijah. In 1 Kings 17, for example, Elijah journeys to Zarephath. Hungry and nearing

dehydration, Elijah requests the help of a poor
widow, and she gives her last meal to this prophet of
God. Powerful things can occur when believers help
each other. Elijah was spared starvation by her faith
in his promise, and she, in turn, was blessed to see
that promise come true:

> "The jar of flour will not be used up and the jug
> of oil will not run dry until the day the LORD
> gives rain on the land." . . . So there was food
> every day for Elijah and for the woman and her
> family (vv. 14, 15).

Powerful things can occur when
believers help each other.

The widow's son, now, grows ill, worsens, and
stops breathing. Elijah cries out in prayer to God
and "the LORD heard Elijah's cry, and the boy's life
returned to him, and he lived" (v. 22). It's no wonder
that James, the brother of Jesus, later urges Christians to pray for the sick and specifically uses Elijah
as his example that "the prayer of a righteous man is
powerful and effective" (James 5:16).

Then comes one of the greatest tests of Elijah's
faith and ministry. His boldness is unparalleled
when he taunts the people: "How long will you waver
between two opinions? If the LORD is God, follow
him; but if Baal is God, follow him" (1 Kings 18:21).
He journeys to the top of Mount Carmel and experiences the presence of God and the angels working on
his behalf.

Read the story in 1 Kings 18. Many times in
Scripture God's angels are associated with wind or

fire. This is one of those "fire" times. Elijah chal-
lenges the prophets of Baal to see whose god will
light the fire under their respective offerings. Elijah
makes it as difficult a test for himself and his God as
he possibly can by completely saturating his altar
and offering with water. Still "the fire of the LORD
fell and burned up the sacrifice, the wood, the stones
and the soil, and also licked up the water in the
trench" (1 Kings 18:38).

God comes through for Elijah. The victory is
complete. When the contest is over, Elijah's God is
obviously the one in charge. Elijah knows it will be
so, even before it occurs. Just as he knows "there is
the sound of a heavy rain" long before that prophecy
becomes a reality (v. 41). Elijah's discernment for
spiritual things is phenomenal.

Yet, even spiritual giants have their down times.
Elijah is no exception. The beautiful element in
Elijah's story is that just as God's angels are with
him in mighty power on the mountain, they are also
with him in gentle whispers in his emotional valley.
Read 1 Kings 19. What a story!

Elijah is spiritually, emotionally, and physically
exhausted. He has nothing left. Have you been
there? This great prophet who's just been empowered by God to pull off one of the most stunning
defeats of evil in history is depressed to the point of
suicide. Look what God does at a moment like that:
"All at once an angel touched him and said, 'Get up
and eat.' He looked around, and there by his head
was a cake of bread baked over hot coals, and a jar of
water" (1 Kings 19: 5, 6).

Home-baked bread. Can you believe it? Remember Grandma's house at Christmas? The savory
smell of baking bread is unequalled. Years ago, our
family loved to drive down Interstate 30 near the

interchange in Fort Worth just to get a "whiff" of the
Mrs. Baird's bread plant. Baking bread. That's what
Elijah smells when he wakes from his depressive
exhaustion. Angels will even bake bread for us if
that's our need at the moment.

The angel doesn't leave Elijah alone, though. The
angel feeds him again, encourages him on his way,
shows him a tremendous display of God's power and
might. Then, the angel gives Elijah the precise word
from God he needs at this moment. It is spoken in a
gentle whisper.

***Angels will even bake bread for us if
that's our need at the moment.***

Out of that word of encouragement, Elijah begins
mentoring a young man named Elisha. What a
match made in heaven that is! The two work side by
side, facing opposition without fear, trusting God to
provide and protect.

Then comes the time for teacher to pass the torch
to student. Having been a teacher for twenty years, I
know that few things are as rewarding as seeing
those you've mentored take the torch and move into
their generation with its power. The story is one of
the most poignant in all Scripture.

Perhaps the most amazing facet of this story
occurs at the time of Elijah's departure:

> As they were walking along and talking together,
> suddenly a chariot of fire and horses of fire
> appeared and separated the two of them, and
> Elijah went up to heaven in a whirlwind (2 Kings
> 2:11).

Angels. Fire. Wind. Here you have all three.

Chariots and horses of fire. I believe that the drivers of these chariots are angelic beings. Then, a whirlwind. And Elijah is gone.

Elisha Follows Elijah

Elisha feels alone. He cries out, "Where now is the LORD, the God of Elijah?" (2 Kings 2:14). Have you ever felt that way? Look what God does for Elisha: "When he struck the water, it divided to the right and to the left, and he crossed over" (2 Kings 2:14). A miraculous crossing of the Jordan, much like Elijah's earlier. Can there be any doubt in Elisha's mind at this point that the God who's been with Elijah will also be with him?

The most powerful moment of this story, however, is yet to come. In 2 Kings 6, Elisha's servant is overwhelmed by the massive forces lined up against God's people. Do you know the feeling? The odds seem insurmountable:

> When the servant of the man of God got up and went out early the next morning, an army with horses and chariots had surrounded the city. "Oh, my lord, what shall we do?" the servant asked.
>
> "Don't be afraid," the prophet answered. "Those who are with us are more than those who are with them."
>
> And Elisha prayed, "O LORD, open his eyes so he may see." Then the LORD opened the servant's eyes, and he looked and saw the hills full of horses and chariots of fire all around Elisha (2 Kings 6:15-17).

What a powerful moment! Our lives cry out to hear the encouraging message: "Those who are with us are more than those who are with them." It's still as true today as it was on that day. Satan and his helpers don't have a prayer.

Surrounded by Strength

Our problem, though, is much like the problem of Elisha's servant. Our spiritual eyes are closed. We need our discernment sharpened; we need our eyes opened so we may see. Like him, we, too, need to see "the hills full of horses and chariots of fire."

When you're feeling as though you could single-handedly conquer the forces of evil on a thousand mountains, don't forget the One who sends the fires of victory.

- Maybe you just graduated from ministerial training;

- Or you've recently signed up for a mission tour;

- Or the couple you've been studying with decided to confess Jesus as their Lord;

- Or rave reviews for your first sermon are in;

- Or you just refused a strong temptation.

Praise God! He provides the power and the poise.

On the other hand, when you're wallowing in depression because the bottom has fallen out of your world, remember the One who provides warm bread and gentle whispers.

- Maybe a Jezebel is after you;

- Or you've just received a word of criticism;

- Or a brother has just written you up in his paper;

- Or you've just done something you swore you would never do;

- Or you can't find a soul to join your cause.

Praise God! He provides the comfort and the consolation.

The heavenly host surrounds us, too, child of God! If we will only believe that. Our God provides just what we need. At times it seems like we need an army to get us out of the messes we make of our lives. They're ready. At other times, we need warm bread and gentle whispers. Praise God! He's capable and willing to provide that, too.

A college student recounts a time when her eyes were opened to see God's strength:

> Late one night while walking across campus, I encountered two suspicious-looking men who were obviously eyeing me and heading toward me when, all of a sudden, they got looks of fear on their faces, stopped, turned, and headed the other way.

> I looked around in an attempt to see what had prompted their hasty departure. No one was there. Not far from me, I saw campus police approach the two and escort them away. They were later charged and convicted of raping a campus coed.

> One of the arresting officers later confided in me that they asked the two why they hadn't bothered me that night. Their reply: "We weren't about to bother her with those two big boyfriends with her." They'd seen two seven-foot-tall men, dressed in white, walking on either side of me. They decided to leave me alone. I saw no one with me. Obviously, however, God was looking after me.

I heard Billy Graham years ago tell of an Indian village which was not attacked by its enemy because of the "huge army which surrounded the village." The villagers saw no one. I never thought when I heard that story that anything similar might someday happen to me. Jehovah is Lord of Hosts!

In contrast to such angel experiences as this, often it is the gentle reminder of God's presence which we desperately seek. My wife, Joan, tells just such a story from her life:

It was Saturday morning, the fifth day of my ordeal. Since Tuesday, I'd been doubled over in pain in a hospital bed. Shots of morphine every four hours alleviated the pain for only two hours at a time, leaving me in severe pain half of each day. IVs strung from my body pumped life-saving antibiotics in hopes of arresting the infection. In spite of all efforts, my white blood count continued to rise. The prognosis was not good.

By Friday night I was depressed, dejected, and wanted to get well and go home. I prayed, asking God for a sign that he was in this with me. I proceeded to inform God as to *precisely* what sign I expected. I wanted the doctor to arrive the next morning with a pill bottle in his hand, a smile on his face, and the words on his lips, "These pills will fix you up. We're sending you home."

Well, he arrived that Saturday morning all right. Bright and early. He carried no pill bottle, but he was followed by a man I knew to be a surgeon. I knew what that meant. They informed me that they'd waited long enough—that things were getting worse, not better. Surgery was scheduled for early the next morning—Sunday. I cried as they left.

Several hours later, the surgeon came back, this time alone. He approached my bed and said, "I wanted to know if you understand about tomorrow. Are you OK?"

"No."

"What's wrong?" he asked.

"I'm afraid," I said.

"Don't you know fear's a sin?" he asked.

Tears ran down my cheeks. "Yes, and that's why I'm so afraid."

"Well, we're going to take care of that right now," he comforted. He invited my mother, who was in the room at the time, to join us in prayer. I've prayed a lot of prayers in my life, but *never* have I had one affect me as that one did. As he prayed it was as if I were floating above my bed. The pain subsided for the first time in days. He left and I told Mom, "God answered my prayer—that was my sign."

Even though the pain returned, the fear did not. I later asked that surgeon why he came back to my room that Saturday to pray. He said he was in his office studying and was *told* to do it. Up to that time, he'd never prayed with a patient.

All I know is that he *became* my sign from God that Saturday almost two decades ago. He was God's messenger—God's angel if you please—to my aching heart. He offered me a comfort and a peace that I'd not known in days.

After the surgery, he informed Larry that the

gall bladder had already perforated and had they waited until Monday to do surgery, the odds of my survival would have drastically decreased.

I cannot tell you the comfort I felt three months later when Larry and I were back at the hospital signing surgical permission papers that read: "Possible radical mastectomy" because of a tumor discovered in my breast. That time I went into surgery knowing that my life was in the hands of not only a master surgeon, but also a prayer partner and friend who walks closely with the Great Physician to comfort and protect me.

Notes

[1]Reuben Slone, *The Light Behind the Cloud* (Waco, Tex.: Texian Press, 1992) 64-81. Used by permission.

Focusing Your Faith:

1. How does pain and distress affect your personal need for God's presence?

2. Put yourself in Elijah's place. Would you have been more acutely aware of God's presence when you ate the bread baked by the widow or by the angel? Why?

3. When has a "widow of Zarephath" provided for you? When has there been an angel making special provision for *your* deepest need?

4. Recall a circumstance that paralyzed you with the same fear that gripped Elisha's servant.

5. Who was your Elisha, who prayed for God to open your eyes to his protection?

6. How does it feel to know that heaven's hosts are on your side?

7. Lay your greatest fear at the throne of God. Ask for deliverance at the hands of his comforting angels.

Daniel 3:16-18

Shadrach, Meshach and Abednego replied to the king, "O Nebuchadnezzar, we do not need to defend ourselves before you in this matter. If we are thrown into the blazing furnace, the God we serve is able to save us from it, and he will rescue us from your hand, O king. But even if he does not, we want you to know, O king, that we will not serve your gods or worship the image of gold you have set up."

Chapter 7

Living in a
Plan B World

Angels Walk Us through the Fire

$\mathcal{A}$ longtime friend and lovely Christian lady, Gatha Longley, tells a riveting story about facing the possible death of her husband:

Around midnight, January 1, 1994, my husband, Bill, began having seizures. I called 911, and an ambulance rushed Bill to the hospital.

The next day I started calling people to begin praying for Bill. We spent the next four to six hours waiting and praying. Soon Bill's organs started shutting down. Then his pupils became fixed and dilated. Bill was dying.

I said to myself, "I still believe in miracles, and I think this is one." Then I thought, "I have to say this out loud." I repeated it aloud. Then I thought, "I've really put God on the spot." At 8:00 A.M. they took Bill to the Neuro ICU. They still couldn't find what was wrong with him.

A mass was soon found in Bill's brain, and the neurosurgeon decided to operate. During the surgery, two types of cancer were found. His doctor explained that he couldn't get all of the cancer and that radiation would be Bill's only hope.

God's Plan A for us was paradise. We rejected that. We live in a Plan B world of our own making.

Bad things do happen in this life. The Bible promises us that. But that is one promise you *won't* hear discussed on the next Health and Wealth Gospel Hour. Cancer will strike. Heart attacks will happen. Deaths of those we love will occur. None of this is as God originally wanted it. God's Plan A for us was paradise. We rejected that. We live in a Plan B world of our own making.

But God can take our Plan B lives and, with the help of his angels, make them better than we ever thought they could be. God's plan A involves the redemption provided by Jesus. Calvary is not an afterthought. God posted his angels at the gate of the Garden so that we'd not eat of the tree of life and live forever in a state of disease and distress. Then, he began preparations for *Gan Eden,* Heaven, where we can enjoy a pain-free environment with him forever. In the meantime, we dwell in the middle—between *Paradise Lost* and *Paradise Regained.* Milton wasn't as blind as they thought.

While we're here, things will occur that God would not have wanted for us. They're often the products of the choices that plunged us into a Plan B world.

The Fires of Life

But, praise God! His angels are by our side, walking through the fires of life with us every step of the way.

God has blessed Joan and me greatly to have lived the better part of two decades across the street from Wade and Emma Felps. Stricken by polio as a child, Emma is as sweet, yet courageous, as anyone I've ever known.

I can't visualize Emma in a "No Fear" T-shirt, but if anyone ever deserved to wear one, it would be this lady. Emma has, over her lifetime, faced enough physical crises to emotionally cripple the stoutest heart. Yet she has faced these situations with genuine bravado.

She defied fear again last year when, at age 67, she fulfilled a prayer of her daughter Sarah by skiing for the first time in beautiful Colorado. As a little girl, Emma had loved to run, but her battle with polio made even walking difficult. Skiing reminded Emma how good it felt to have the wind racing through her hair just as it had as a child.

In spite of her courage, Emma tells of a time several years ago when God walked her through the fire of fear and helplessness. How God chose to do that is a priceless story.

A number of years ago I was in a recovery area of a local hospital following major surgery. My family had left the hospital after their last visiting time. My pain continued and the staff could not seem to help me. In the late evening my bed was pushed to a curtained area. I could no longer see the nurses, nor could they see me without walking a distance from their station. I had no way to ring for a nurse, no telephone, and no one

could see me. Nighttime rounds were far apart,
and visiting hours were long past, so I knew my
family wouldn't be looking for me. In my pain and
separation I became anxious. I knew how weak
and helpless I was, and felt completely alone.

I have no idea what time it was, but I was wide
awake and prayerful when a most unusual thing
happened. The curtain near the head of my bed
parted and my friend Bob Hamm appeared. I
couldn't believe it; he was like an angel. He spoke
words of comfort and hope, and then the curtains
closed. How could this be? It was very late at
night, but I knew I was not dreaming. I relaxed
and knew I'd be all right. Needless to say, this
did more for me than any medication!

What caused Bob to make this unexpected visit
to Emma's recovery room in the middle of the night?
Bob tells this remarkable story:

I was driving down the freeway late one night in
a hurry, headed for home. Suddenly I had an urge
to turn off and go by the hospital to see Emma,
but I kept driving on down the freeway. I told
myself I was tired, and besides, visiting hours
were over. Emma was probably asleep anyway.

It was not until I had received another *strong*
nudge, that I turned off and went to the hospital. I
found the area where Emma was supposed to be,
but she wasn't there. I insisted that I must see
her, as an elder of her church. After some time
they took me to her well-hidden bed and permit-
ted a brief visit. I don't understand the strong
urge that came over me to make that hospital call,
but I know it was the right thing for me to do.

To this day, Emma sees God's hand in the events

of that night, getting her through a fiery situation in which her paralysis had not been polio, but fear. It's amazing what God can still do today through Christians who are sensitive to his angels' strong nudgings!

The Fiery Furnace

Two familiar Bible stories that also illustrate this point are found in the Book of Daniel. The first is in 3:12-29. Shadrach, Meshach, and Abednego are deeply dedicated servants of God. They are not about to give way to public pressure, to bow down and worship a god of gold when Yahweh is their God.

Displeased with their unwillingness to bow to the pressures, the king threatens to annihilate them to prove to the community that he is serious about his edict. They confidently respond: "If we are thrown into the blazing furnace, the God we serve is able to save us from it, and he will rescue us from your hand, O king. But even if he does not, we want you to know, O king, that we will not serve your gods or worship the image of gold you have set up" (vv. 17, 18). Case closed.

Health and Wealth proclaimers would condemn anyone who'd utter a faithless statement like "even if he does not." How can they expect a miracle if they don't believe one might happen? Their words, according to these people, betray their lack of faith. No wonder these three went through the fire.

I disagree. I believe the "even if he does not" phrase is the essence of pure faith. My commitment is to God, no matter what occurs. I'm not in this thing for the rewards. Whatever happens, God's hands are the best hands to be in.

The next thing they know, they are standing in the flames. But they are not alone: "Look! I see four men walking around in the fire" (v. 25). The angelic

protection extended by God is so effective that upon
their exit, "the fire had not harmed their bodies, nor
was a hair of their heads singed; their robes were
not scorched, and there was no smell of fire on them"
(v. 27). How's that for protection? Later, even the
king recognizes the faithfulness of God to his people
and declares: "Praise be to the God of Shadrach,
Meshach and Abednego, who has sent his angel and
rescued his servants!"

The Lions' Den

Daniel's second faith story, from Daniel 6:7-23, is
equally gripping. "Now when Daniel learned that the
decree had been published, he went home . . . and
prayed . . . just as he had done before" (v. 10). No
threat of death is about to deter Daniel. Prayer to his
God is a vital part of his day. That will not change for
anyone's decree. So, Daniel ends up spending the
night with some hungry lions. Yet, God's passion to
prove himself faithful to his servant Daniel is the
most powerful force at work that night, and Daniel's
angelic house guest saves the day: "My God sent his
angel, and he shut the mouths of the lions" (v. 22).

Several years ago I heard of a basketball coach
who forfeited a state playoff game because of his
discovery that twins on his team had switched jer-
seys when the better player fouled out. The switch
allowed the better player to unfairly finish the game,
winning it for the team.

For his integrity, the small town, where basketball was taken seriously, treated this man as if he
were Public Enemy Number One. His house was
sprayed with graffiti. His car tires were slashed. His
wife and children were accosted in public. His family
was quite literally driven out of town. The price tag
of integrity is often quite high in our society.

In the Heart of the Fire

Life, at times, will be unfair and unjust. For unexplainable reasons some people will take us on as their personal destruction projects. Laws will be passed to punish those who are trying to do what's right. We'll be accused, interrogated, tried, condemned, and sentenced—all in the name of justice.

At such times it will appear as though evil has triumphed—like we're the big losers. At times like that, look at the faithfulness flowing in these stories.

If your definition of God's faithfulness requires that he spare us completely from the fires and lions' dens of life, then these two stories are not going to help you very much. These two stories have great endings compared to some others. Angels don't always keep people from dying. They seemed to be present at Stephen's stoning. Yet, he died. Onlookers at the burning of Polycarp, bishop of Smyrna, were convinced of angelic activity surrounding his execution, yet he, too, died.

Angel activity does not exempt us from life's struggles and difficulties. We are not delivered from all injustices. Life does not become suddenly fair. And what we, from an earthly perspective, would consider happy endings will not always be the result of God's angels interacting with us.

What, then, do these two stories tell us? We learn that, while God's angels do not always deliver us *from* the fires of life, they do walk with us *through* those fires.

Have you ever felt alone in your pain? You weren't. Even if it felt like you were. Have you felt as though no one could possibly understand? They do. Even if it seems they couldn't. Does it seem that no one is there for you? They are. Even if you can't see them. They're called angels. And, among their other responsibilities, angels are in the heart of life's worst fires with us to make certain that our spirits aren't scorched.

Angels are in the heart of life's worst fires with us to make certain that our spirits aren't scorched.

Notice that I said our spirits. They are angels' primary interest. Our bodies are only secondary. If not a hair of our physical heads is scorched, as was the case with Shadrach and friends, praise God! He obviously has further plans for us here.

Yet, we must remember that Stephen and Polycarp were no worse off than these three. Death is not defeat for the believer. Without fear, Polycarp lifted his hand in the air and said, "My God has stood beside me all these years. He'll not desert me now." Polycarp was right. God's angels took him home.

The basketball coach that I spoke of earlier had quite a surprise awaiting him several years later when one of the twins, the poorer player, approached him while visiting the coach's church. It seems that the boy could not put out of his mind the courage and integrity the coach had displayed through all the evil things that happened to him. The boy wanted to know more about this Jesus who made such a difference in the coach's life.

Returning to our first story in this chapter, Gatha Longley prayed for a miracle—that God would have further plans on earth for her dying husband, Bill:

A man came up to me in the crowded Neuro Unit

waiting room. He had white hair, blue eyes, and was wearing jeans. He told me he had a message for me. He said, "This is a miracle. Don't think I'm crazy."

"I don't," I said.

He said it was important that the elders of our church pray over Bill either that night or the next. I explained that people had been praying for him, but he said the men needed to lay hands on Bill and said that he wanted to pray over Bill, also. I told him it would be done. He told me to trust in God and depend on my friends. He repeated it again. Then he glanced around the room and left.

I called our minister and told him what happened, and he assured me it would be done.

In the Neuro Unit, only two people were allowed in at one time to see the patient, but the nurse on duty made an exception. My group of friends could go in, but not the unknown man.

When the men arrived that night, our minister anointed Bill with oil, and each man prayed over him.

When I went in to see Bill for my first visit following surgery, I saw an envelope addressed to me underneath our family picture. I opened it and read, "Dear Gatha, trust in God. Let your friends help you, for in doing so, they will receive a greater blessing." It continued, "I prayed over Bill this morning." Then the note listed Scripture references: Proverbs 3:5-8; Psalm 28:6, 7; Psalm 37:5; Psalm 62:5, 8. It was signed, "A Servant of God." When I asked the nurse if anyone had been in Bill's room, she said no.

Bill's room was located next to the nurse's station. There was a window between his room and the station, and a person had to pass the nurse's station to get to his room. Those entering must press a button, announce themselves, and request entry. No one had done so. I asked if someone could have handed the letter to a nurse who, in turn, placed it in Bill's room. She said the letter would have been registered and placed outside the room next to the door, not inside as it was. The nurse became concerned, but I said, "Don't worry, I think I know who it is."

As I contemplated these events and the mysterious messenger, I felt confident that I had encountered an angel.

Two months later, the unknown man called me at home when Bill was in rehabilitation. He said the elders must again pray over Bill, to get rid of the cancer. Three nights later, the men prayed over Bill once again.

Bill's CAT scan in May, then his MRI in December of that year showed no trace of a tumor. The evidences seem clear that my husband is cured.

Dr. Raymond Kelsey, my Bible professor at Oklahoma Christian University, once said he felt there were times when heaven and earth crossed paths. I feel this has been one of those times.

We are never alone when it's time to walk through the fires of life. God and his angels, whether visible or invisible, are always there, either to rescue us or escort us. In the end, our souls will arrive at the throne of God unscorched.

Focusing Your Faith:

1. Do you think it was fair for God to allow Shadrach, Meshach, and Abednego to be placed in a fiery furnace? Why?

2. Whose fiery furnace trial have you witnessed? Did they praise or blame God for it?

3. As you observed their experience, was your faith strengthened or weakened? Why?

4. How equipped are you to walk through a "fiery furnace"?

5. What do you suppose would happen to your faith if you went through such trial? Do you think your response would encourage or discourage the faith of others?

6. How do angels involve themselves in our trials of life?

7. Think of someone currently in life's fiery furnace. Pray that _you_ will be empowered to be their angel of encouragement.

Matthew 4:1-11

Then Jesus was led by the Spirit into the desert to be tempted by the devil. After fasting forty days and forty nights, he was hungry. The tempter came to him and said, "If you are the Son of God, tell these stones to become bread."

Jesus answered, "It is written: 'Man does not live on bread alone, but on every word that comes from the mouth of God.' "

Then the devil took him to the holy city and had him stand on the highest point of the temple. "If you are the Son of God," he said, "throw yourself down. For it is written:

'He will command his angels concerning you,
    and they will lift you up in their hands,
so that you will not strike your foot against a stone.' "

Jesus answered him, "It is also written: 'Do not put the Lord your God to the test.' "

Again, the devil took him to a very high mountain and showed him all the kingdoms of the world and their splendor. "All this I will give you," he said, "if you will bow down and worship me."

Jesus said to him, "Away from me, Satan! For it is written: 'Worship the Lord your God, and serve him only.' "

Then the devil left him, and angels came and attended him.

Chapter 8

When Desert Winds Blow

Angels Act in Our Best Interest

A troubled young man just left my counseling office. His story is so similar to the many I see each week. He is a Christian, yet he struggles with impure thoughts. He knows he shouldn't. He doesn't want to. But he can't seem to make himself stop. He reminds me a lot of the apostle Paul when he laments, "The evil I do not want to do—this I keep on doing" (Romans 7:19).

Of course there were some life skills that I could help this young man develop, yet the most helpful advice I could possibly offer him was for him to familiarize himself with the many passages of Scripture that deal with the temptations that dog our paths.

I don't know about you, but I know in my life, temptations, tests, and trials are virtually daily occurrences. I don't like them. I'd just as soon live life without them. But they appear to be here to stay.

My wife, Joan, had a terrifying bout with temporary blindness as a result of her diabetes, which brought us to our knees and to our senses. Among other things, our rebirth from these events has resulted in our loss of a combined 130 pounds. We can only praise God for that.

Thanks to Joan's diabetes and the daily regimen it demands from both of us, with God's help, I hope never again to be a 250-pound preacher spending all my pulpit time pouncing on the weaknesses which cause others to yield to temptation. It's high time for us fat preachers to stop behaving as though we have no weaknesses.

We all have temptations that plague us. Yours may be one thing. Hers, another. One of my biggest temptations throughout my adult life has been the temptation to overeat. The heat of the scorching winds of that temptation have been as destructive in my life as your trials are to you. And the consequences, every bit as devastating.

When such times come, it helps to contemplate such passages as, "When tempted, no one should say, 'God is tempting me.' For God cannot be tempted by evil, nor does he tempt anyone; but each one is tempted when, by his own evil desire, he is dragged away and enticed" (James 1:13, 14). That passage may be uncomfortable, but it at least reminds me of two important truths:

1. I shouldn't blame God;

2. Ultimately, the choice is mine.

A passage that helps me even more is found in 1 Corinthians 10:13: "No temptation has seized you except what is common to man. And God is faithful; he will not let you be tempted beyond what you can bear. But when you are tempted, he will also provide a way out so that you can stand up under it." Wow! I can sink my teeth into that verse. It tells me . . .

- others have similar trials;

- God is faithful (even if you feel like he isn't);

- he will not overload us (even if we feel like he has);

- he will provide a way out (even if you feel like he hasn't);

- he knows we can bear up under it (even if we feel like we can't).

But of all the passages concerning temptation, I think *the* most meaningful to me is Hebrews 4:15: "For we do not have a high priest who is unable to sympathize with our weaknesses, but we have one who has been tempted in every way, just as we are—yet was without sin." That verse tells me that Jesus understands my temptations. And knowing someone *really* understands means more than all the other verses put together.

If we ever have a moment when we doubt the truth of Hebrews 4:15, we need to take a close look at Matthew 4:1-11:

Then Jesus was led by the Spirit into the desert to be tempted by the devil. After fasting forty days and forty nights, he was hungry. The tempter came to him and said, "If you are the Son of God, tell these stones to become bread." Jesus answered, "It is written: 'Man does not live on bread alone, but on every word that comes from the mouth of God.' "

Then the devil took him to the holy city and had him stand on the highest point of the temple. "If you are the Son of God," he said, "throw yourself down. For it is written:

'He will command his angels concerning you,
    and they will lift you up in their hands,
so that you will not strike your foot against a
        stone.' "

Jesus answered him, "It is also written: 'Do not put the Lord your God to the test.' "

Again, the devil took him to a very high mountain and showed him all the kingdoms of the world and their splendor. "All this I will give you," he said, "if you will bow down and worship me."

Jesus said to him, "Away from me, Satan! For it is written: 'Worship the Lord your God, and serve him only.' "

Then the devil left him, and angels came and attended him.

The Purpose of Trials

The first thing that "jumps off the page" at us in this passage is that, while God does not do the tempting, it is the Holy Spirit who leads Jesus into the desert for the specific purpose of being tempted by Satan. Why is that? I think in regard to Jesus the answer is unique to him personally. Jesus is on his way to becoming our faithful high priest. The journey there necessitates his being "tempted in every way just as we are." No short cuts. No bargain-basement quick fix. For Jesus to return to the Father's right hand to become the One who pleads our case, he has to travel through an arid desert of temptation and overcome an excruciating cross of pain and separation from God.

But why would God allow us to go through similar deserts of temptation in our lives? Obviously, we aren't working to become high priests. For us, it is a matter of character development. The hot desert winds blowing across our lives strengthen our resolve, sharpen our courage, and heighten our reliance upon God. We leave the desert better and stronger for having struggled against its winds.

The hot desert winds blowing across our lives strengthen our resolve, sharpen our courage, and heighten our reliance upon God.

The Fallen Angel

We learn a great deal in this passage about the enemy, the fallen angel, the devil. Because Satan is not omnipresent, he cannot be everywhere. He is not deity. Therefore, he, unlike God, is limited to being in one place at a time.

While this prompts him to employ his demons (other fallen angels) from time to time to do his bidding, he evidently handled Jesus' temptation in Matthew 4 personally. Facing the Son of God himself would certainly require calling out the big guns and pulling out all the stops.

Notice, however, that Satan is no match for Jesus. Later in the New Testament we read "greater is he that is in you, than he that is in the world" (1 John 4:4, KJV). In this account of Jesus' temptations, we see it graphically. Satan cannot order Jesus. Satan cannot dictate to Jesus. Satan cannot bargain with Jesus as he would with an equal.

Satan waits to attack until Jesus reaches his physically weakest, most vulnerable point—forty days and nights without food. Jesus is hungry. Satan operates that way. He watches carefully to see us in our most vulnerable moment, then he attacks.

The Temptations

When Satan attacks, his strategy with us is much the same as with Jesus. Just as novelists concur that only a limited number of basic plots exist on which to build a novel, so three basic avenues of temptation exist: the lust of the flesh, the lust of the eyes, and the pride of life. Satan is a master strategist at those because they cost him his place in heaven.

I counsel people struggling with these three types of temptations every day. Let me share with you in more recognizable terms what I believe Jesus' temptations to be. By understanding these, we can better deal with the tricks of the fallen angel who attacks us.

1. You can do it yourself. Satan says to Jesus, "Come on now. You can do this. You're hungry. You have the power. Solve your dilemma. Make yourself supper out of these rocks. No problem! Right?"

Jesus' curt reply is "Wrong!" You see, Jesus understands what we too often forget. Jesus knows well his daily dependence upon the Father for spiritual sustenance and refreshment. That Father-Son relationship is a daily necessity with him—more important than eating bread. Jesus needs his Father, and *knows* it.

Doesn't Satan come after us in similar fashion? He doesn't come at us head-on and try to get us to quit. Instead, he subtly convinces us that we can succeed under our own power. Our programs. Our solutions. Our deeds. Satan's not fearful of a few genuine successes on our part. In fact, those can play right into his hand. They help convince us that we are right—we can go it alone.

The fact is, we can't. Without God as an active participant in our plans, they are ultimately doomed to failure. Proverbs 16:3 says: "Commit to the LORD whatever you do, and your plans will succeed." If Satan can keep us relying on our own strength and ingenuity, he has us right where he wants us. Jesus understands this.

2. If God really loves you, he owes you a rescue. Satan says to Jesus, "If you are the Son of God, claim your scriptural promise." He then quotes Psalm 91:11, 12. Satan can quote Scripture if it plays toward his goals. "God owes you. He can't let you fall. His angels *must* rescue you. He promised." Satan thinks he has God boxed up by his own promises.

Jesus' reply is simple: "Do not test the Lord your God" (Deuteronomy 6:16). Jesus also quotes Scripture, you see.

Isn't this Satanic ploy a big gun in the devil's arsenal? "If you're really a Christian, everything should go well with you. No problems. No rain on your parade. No clouds in your sky. No thorns on your rosebush. Claim your promise. Believe strong. Pray hard. God owes you."

Then when the first hint of a problem occurs in our lives, Satan returns, either to remind us of our own failures: "You didn't do it right. You should've believed harder. You should've prayed more." Or, to remind us of God's "failures": "He doesn't really love you. How could a good God let this happen? I told you so. He's out to get you. He doesn't really care about you."

Jesus refuses to allow this whole scenario to develop. He brings it to a quick end by saying, in essence, "Look, Satan, I believe in my Father no matter what. I don't have to throw myself off a wall to prove him. He loves me. I know that. Even if I crashed on the ground and became a cripple, it would not change the fact that he loves me. If I were to die, he'd simply take me home to be with him. You're not going to get me to give my Father a test. He's already more than passed."

3. ***What's it worth to you?*** Satan's third strategy has to do with worth. "See all this splendor? What's it worth to you? I'll give it to you if you'll worship me."

Worship, you see, is about worth. *Worth-ship*. When I worship someone or something, I'm declaring their worth to my life. Satan wants our worship. He wants us to declare him worthy.

Yet, the angelic cry throughout Revelation rings out, "Worthy is the Lamb!" And here the Lamb of God, Jesus, is saying, "Worship the Lord your God and serve him only." Jesus boldly declares his pledge of allegiance.

We must realize that we don't have to become Satanists to be guilty of stumbling into this third avenue of temptation. All we have to do is set our eyes so intently on the splendor of this world that it mesmerizes us and becomes the primary focus of our lives.

Jesus later warns us in Mark how easy it is to gain the whole world and lose our souls. How many dads have sacrificed their families on the altar of corporate success? How many husbands have destroyed their marriages through the pursuit of momentary pleasures?

Just yesterday I had a divorced couple in my

office whose teenager is in rebellion. It seems that six years ago, Dad's six-figure salary prompted him to pursue a freer lifestyle than marriage would allow. "I just want to have fun" was his cry.

Now he's crying, all right, but for a different reason. His daughter has decided to follow in Dad's footsteps. What one generation perceives themselves to be doing in moderation, the next generation tends to do in excess. Thanks to Dad's selfishness, this family has some pretty rough years ahead of it.

We sacrifice our all on the altar of more, bigger, faster, and better, demonstrating that we have decided what we think is really worthy in our lives.

Sometimes we forget what's really important, and we attribute too much worth to the material things in this world. Then we sacrifice our all on the altar of more, bigger, faster, and better, demonstrating that we have decided what we think is really worthy in our lives.

Yet, the truth remains: He alone is worthy.

The Angels Arrive

Finally, the temptations end, at least for now. The devil leaves. And look who arrives to serve Jesus: Angels!

What a picture! Though we have no details, I envision this scene much like the time when angels baked Elijah bread, gave him water, watched over his sleep, comforted, nursed, consoled, encouraged, and helped him. I think they did all this for Jesus, too.

Someone might ask, "But where were they when

he needed them—in the heat of the temptation?" The answer is, "Right there beside him."

"Then why didn't they do something?"

They probably did.

"I mean, why didn't they stop it from happening?"

That's not what angels do.

"Why didn't Jesus call for help?"

Probably for the same reason that he would not call for legions of angels to deliver him from being crucified.

Going It Alone

Some times in life are neither for calling nor expecting angelic deliverance. Sometimes you face it alone. But don't be afraid. You're never really alone, even if you feel like you are.

My daughter, Lisa, shares a chilling story of a woman facing death alone on a busy highway.

Last year, one of my dearest friends in the world, a sweet Christian lady named Lynn, was killed in a tragic auto accident. Her husband and sons had never shared her deep spiritual commitment. That was always a concern of hers. We had talked about it often.

Shortly after her death, a lady called the family home and insisted upon talking to Lynn's husband. Relating details of Lynn only a witness could know, she told him that she had arrived at the scene as the accident occurred and had held Lynn in her arms during those first few moments following the accident.

She told the husband that Lynn asked her to pray with her and that Lynn did the praying. According to the lady, Lynn's prayer was not for herself nor her salvation, but that God would work in her sons' and husband's lives. The lady said that Lynn was secure in her salvation. She added that she had promised Lynn that she'd make this phone call, and that's why she wouldn't give up until she'd talked with Lynn's husband personally.

The unusual thing about this story is that one of Lynn's sons was traveling on the same highway as Lynn, literally just seconds behind her. He arrived on the accident scene very shortly after it occurred. Yet, neither he nor any other passersby saw this mysterious lady.

Whoever she was, she blessed this family by her call, because Lynn's husband, who'd seldom set foot in a church building, has missed few Sundays since the lady's call.

While working on this book, I discovered that one of our freelance editors, Becky King, was also on that road the day of the accident. In fact, except for going back into her house to retrieve a pair of shoes she'd forgotten, Becky would have been precisely at the place where the sleeping driver had slammed into Lynn's car.

Some forty-five seconds behind the accident, Becky watched as Lynn's son jumped out of his truck and frantically, but unsuccessfully, tried to open the car's locked doors. Seeing the mangled car, Becky felt little hope for the driver's survival. As she stayed in her car, she prayed that God would comfort the driver and her family in her death. She prayed at *precisely* the moment identified by the mysterious caller as being the time when the caller was holding Lynn in her arms and praying with her. As we ask, God is already answering.

Whatever our need, wherever we are, whenever it's time, God's angels are acting in our best interest . . . ultimately. They may not save us from the immediate disaster; rather, they will support us through life's tough times in order to save us from eternal disaster. Praise God for his angelic servants, who lead us safely through the windy, searing desert we call life.

Focusing Your Faith:

1. Is the source of your temptations internal or external? Why?

2. Do you believe the temptations of this century are greater than the temptations faced by Jesus? Why?

3. How does Hebrews 4:15 fit with this comparison?

4. Why would the Spirit lead Jesus into the desert to be tempted? Why would he lead us into *our* deserts?

5. Describe how Satan tempts you in the same ways he tempted Christ.

6. When did Jesus summon the assistance of angels during the temptation in the desert? Would you do the same? Why?

7. Pray for God to provide you with the exact words to banish Satan the next time he confronts you with temptation.

Matthew 17:1-9

After six days Jesus took with him Peter, James and John the brother of James, and led them up a high mountain by themselves. There he was transfigured before them. His face shone like the sun, and his clothes became as white as the light. Just then there appeared before them Moses and Elijah, talking with Jesus.

Peter said to Jesus, "Lord, it is good for us to be here. If you wish, I will put up three shelters—one for you, one for Moses and one for Elijah."

While he was still speaking, a bright cloud enveloped them, and a voice from the cloud said, "This is my Son, whom I love; with him I am well pleased. Listen to him!"

When the disciples heard this, they fell facedown to the ground, terrified. But Jesus came and touched them. "Get up," he said. "Don't be afraid." When they looked up, they saw no one except Jesus.

As they were coming down the mountain, Jesus instructed them, "Don't tell anyone what you have seen, until the Son of Man has been raised from the dead."

Chapter 9

Cheers from the Grandstand!

Angels Join Those on Our Side

Gary Stolz, a good friend of my secretary, Maureen Verett, has spent most of his adult life in ministry. Having a heart for adolescents, Gary currently works with troubled teens. Gary has fond memories of his grandmother, especially some events which occurred following her death:

> Growing up in a Christian home has afforded many fond memories for me, one of the most cherished being my grandmother, "Mawmaw."

> Ina Mae Stolz was a beautiful Christian woman and devoted wife. Everybody loved her. She loved God, people, and delighted in sharing her steadfast faith and extraordinary love. For years she taught her Priceless Personality Course, designed to help young women become "young ladies" while growing up in the faith.

> From the time I was a child, whenever I stayed

with Mawmaw, she would come into my bedroom every morning, gently rub my back and quietly sing, "Oh, what a beautiful morning. . . ." My family and I smile as we remember those times. She knew singing wasn't her gift, but that didn't matter to us, and it didn't deter her.

Several years ago, I lived with Mawmaw for a while. Then, sadly, the inevitable day arrived when she went Home. "Pawpaw" had passed away only four months earlier. I believe she simply missed him. Our consolation was knowing she would be happy to finally be with her beloved Lord and reunited with Pawpaw.

Mawmaw's personality was reflected everywhere in her home. It was comforting. I continued to live there for some time. One morning, I was roused from my sleep by someone gently rubbing my back, coupled with the strains of that familiar song . . . Mawmaw's voice. I sat up, somewhat confused. Was I dreaming? Time gave the answer. During ensuing months, when those loving hands and that sweet voice woke me from my sleep I knew it was neither a dream nor my imagination.

I firmly believe, as in Hebrews 12:1, that we are "surrounded by such a great cloud of witnesses." I believe Mawmaw, along with many other loved ones, is cheering me on in the heavenly stands, as I "press on toward the goal." I look forward to seeing her again one day. And knowing Mawmaw, she'll continue her time-honored tradition by waking me to the melody of "Oh, what a beautiful morning" . . . forever.

Stories like this one are a little frightening to us

because they go beyond the realm of angel stories. Yet such testimonials come from good, decent, sane, intelligent, Bible-believing people who've made no conscious effort to experience such events. It seems only wise to acknowledge and, at least, examine such occurrences.

Two passages from the Gospels have probably prompted more discussions of the unseen world than any others. One concerns guardian angels, the other, the state of the dead. This chapter will focus on these two intriguing issues.

Guardian Angels

Jesus says it in passing, almost matter-of-factly. He is addressing an issue that remains close to his heart. Jesus wants children and those young in their faith treated right. Child abuse, neglect, or mistreatment of the innocent and naive are beyond Christ's capacity to tolerate. He addresses these issues on several occasions. In Matthew 18:10, however, comes one of his most poignant messages. I especially like this paraphrased version: "Watch that you don't treat a single one of these childlike believers arrogantly. You realize, don't you, that their personal angels are constantly in touch with my Father in heaven?" (TM).

The Case For

Some argue that no idea as widely accepted as guardian angels should be based on any single passage alone. Rightly or wrongly, that is precisely what happens here. Whereas Scripture devotes a great deal of space to discussing angelic intervention and protection, this is the only place in Scripture where the implication is that a one-on-one equation may exist: personal angels.

The matter-of-fact manner in which Jesus refers to personal angels gives guardian-angel advocates the idea that it's a foregone conclusion—an accepted fact. He doesn't explain. He doesn't debate. He doesn't defend. In his discourse on treating folks right, he simply states what he believes to be an important reason why.

So, while it might be stretching it some to grow an entire "movement" out of this passage, it certainly seems reasonable to accept Jesus' simple words at face value.

The Case Against

Those who do not believe in personal guardian angels argue that it really seems to our advantage not to do so. To them it seems much more comforting to think that the entire heavenly host is at our instantaneous disposal rather than only one angel.

Such people obviously believe that their case is a multiangel sort of case. They might do well to pause and realize that perhaps they're giving too much power to their personal problems and too little credit to the awesome power of one angel. Besides, just because we have a personal angel doesn't necessarily mean God can't call an entire angel army if we need it.

The Bottom Line

The point of all this is that God calls his angels to protect and help us. I'm willing to leave it up to him whether he chooses to do that through specific assignments or on an as-needed basis. As long as I begin each day knowing that I'm not living it alone— that God and his angels are watching over me and standing beside me—I can deal with each day's difficulties.

The Dead

Another passage in the Gospels that has prompted a great deal of speculation about the unseen world is the story found in Matthew 17:1-9 that we've come to call the Transfiguration:

Six days later, three of them saw that glory. Jesus took Peter and the brothers, James and John, and led them up a high mountain. His appearance changed from the inside out, right before their eyes. Sunlight poured from his face. His clothes were filled with light. Then they realized that Moses and Elijah were also there in deep conversation with him.

Peter broke in, "Master, this is a great moment! What would you think if I built three memorials here on the mountain—one for you, one for Moses, one for Elijah?"

While he was going on like this, babbling, a light-radiant cloud enveloped them, and sounding from deep in the cloud a voice: "This is my Son, marked by my love, focus of my delight. Listen to him."

When the disciples heard it, they fell flat on their faces, scared to death. But Jesus came over and touched them. "Don't be afraid." When they opened their eyes and looked around all they saw was Jesus, only Jesus.

Coming down the mountain, Jesus swore them to secrecy. "Don't breathe a word of what you've seen. After the Son of Man is raised from the dead, you are free to talk" (TM).

What exactly is going on here? That's the question that haunts us as we read this familiar story.

First of all, it's important to note that this is not an angel story. The spirits of the dead are precisely that: the spirits of the dead. They are not angels.

Numerous passages warn us of the dangers of attempting to contact the other side. Spiritism, séances, witchcraft, and such practices are strongly condemned in Scripture. It's very likely that King Saul's dabbling in such occult activity led directly to his mental collapse and suicide. So when dealing with this subject, care and caution must be exercised.

Still, Jesus offers us, along with Peter, James, and John, a glimpse into eternity. During Jesus' transfiguration, the three disciples preview Jesus as he will become following his resurrection, and they witness the close interaction between heaven and earth. It's as if an invisible wall is all that separates heaven from earth—a permeable corridor from one dimension to another.

The Heavenlies and the Afterlife

I think of the heavenlies in terms of dimension, not direction. That helps me personally. In the long run, what difference will it make precisely how the Lord chooses to return and claim us for eternity? In the meantime, if it helps to think of the heavenlies as being merely an arm's-reach away, as opposed to being somewhere way out beyond the Milky Way and the Black Hole, isn't it appropriate to utilize that metaphor? At best, we are finite beings trying to comprehend infinite reality. Any picture we use will fall short. That's the nature of dealing with eternal matters.

Let me share with you my personal view of the afterlife. I realize that it will not be universally accepted. So be it. I would not impose my views on anyone else, yet what I'm about to share has been helpful to my Jesus walk.

My view of the afterlife grows out of Hebrews 12. In his chapter 11, the writer has introduced us to what I call the Faith Hall of Fame. He has defined *faith* for us, instructed us concerning its importance, and shared with us a directory of great Old Testament heroes of faith—people like Noah, Abraham, Isaac, Jacob, Joseph, Moses, David, and others. Then, on the heels of this, he opens Hebrews 12 with these exciting words:

> Do you see what this means—all these pioneers who blazed the way, all these veterans cheering us on? It means we'd better get on with it. Strip down, start running—and never quit! No extra spiritual fat, no parasitic sins. Keep your eyes on *Jesus*, who both began and finished this race we're in (vv. 1, 2, TM).

Does that metaphor grab you like it does me? Life is a race—a marathon, for sure, but a race nonetheless. We are the runners.

If we'll simply glance into the grandstands, we'll see familiar smiling faces. Noah cheering us on. Abraham shouting, "Hang in there!" Moses yelling, "Don't quit!" David encouraging, "You're gonna win!" What a picture! The Hebrew writer says that such encouragement should spur us on to do our best. I agree.

While dead souls do not become angels, I do believe they join the ranks of those who are on the other side of the sheer curtain that separates this world from the next. I believe that those of our loved ones who've died are right there in the stands cheering us on every step of the way. My dad may be standing right next to Abraham. I hope so. Abraham was always one of Dad's favorite Bible characters.

I do not believe in so-called "soul sleep" in the classical sense. I believe that those who've died are alert and aware of what's going on here. I think the Transfiguration teaches that. I think Hebrews 12 teaches that. I think the story of the rich man and Lazarus teaches that.

Those of our loved ones who've died are right there in the stands cheering us on every step of the way.

I never make attempts to "contact" the dead through spiritist means for fear I'll end up like King Saul. Yet, in a positive way, I do believe that I can converse with my dad. And I believe he hears me. That realization, growing out of Hebrews 12, has been a real blessing during my grief following Dad's death.

In my counseling practice, it seems that those who bring a belief that no awareness exists on the other side of death have the most difficulty processing through their grief. They have unresolved issues, and nowhere to take them. When I introduce them to Hebrews 12, it's like a load is lifted. "D'ya mean my wife might be in those stands, too?" You bet! What a blessing!

Well, there you have it. The "Reader's Digest" condensed version of my theology of the afterlife. I hope it can be as helpful to you as the following story by my good friend Steve Papagno has been to me. How in the world could we allow our fears to paralyze us when God is so actively at work assuring us, as you'll see in Steve's account:

My grandparents, Ed and Oma Sharp, loved each other very much. Their love for each other and everyone they knew, made them two of the finest Christians I've ever known. Their faith was simple, practical, conservative, and biblical. I went to live with them when my granddad became ill with cancer, and I continued to live with Grannie after his passing.

One evening, weeks after the funeral, Grannie and I had returned from a family member's wedding. This was the first one she had attended without Granddad, and she was feeling real low. I was in my room and heard the floor creaking in the hall just as it always did when Granddad walked from the den to his bedroom. I looked up at the doorway and thought I had actually seen him walk by. I didn't know what to think until I heard Grannie talking to someone in her bedroom.

I went down the hallway into Grannie's doorway, and there she sat on her bed, Granddad sitting in his chair in the corner. She motioned me into the room to sit next to her on the bed. Stunned, I sat and savored the moment. Granddad spoke and told Grannie that everything was all right and that she would be fine. The three of us were together again as so many times before. It was not a hallucination. He was there. Not in a physical body, but in a visual presence. Then as quickly as he came, he got up and left the room.

The next morning as I went into the kitchen, my grannie smiled and said, "What did you think about last night?"

I returned the smile and said, "That was something." Not another word was spoken about that night. Yet, she knew it had happened. And so did

I. We didn't seek it. No spiritism or witchcraft were involved.

The only explanation that seems reasonable to me is that God chose to allow Grannie to see that everything was all right with Granddad. He had taken a journey that she has since taken herself. Now they are reunited—eternally.

I think from time to time God chooses, for whatever reason, to give us a glimpse of eternity. I, for one, will be ever grateful for that night with Granddad.

There's no doubt about it—not in my mind anyway: angels and spirits of our friends and family are cheering us on as we complete the race of life. And every time one of God's runners crosses the finish line into heaven, a mighty roar of joy resounds through the hills of eternity.

Thank you, God, for the encouragement and assurance coming from those heavenly grandstands.

Focusing Your Faith:

1. What point does Jesus make in Matthew 18:10? If you take it seriously, how will it affect your attitude toward children?

2. What is *your* position in the guardian angels debate? Why?

3. What reassures you most about God's protective care?

4. How would you describe to a new believer, unfamiliar with the Bible, what occurred at the Transfiguration?

5. Have you ever thought you heard someone cheering you on from celestial grandstands?

6. Describe your picture of the afterlife of loved ones who've died. How has reading this chapter changed that picture?

7. Pray specifically for someone you know who is grieving the death of a loved one. Ask God for words of encouragement to share with that person.

Luke 22:41-45

He withdrew about a stone's throw beyond them, knelt down and prayed, "Father, if you are willing, take this cup from me; yet not my will, but yours be done." An angel from heaven appeared to him and strengthened him. And being in anguish, he prayed more earnestly, and his sweat was like drops of blood falling to the ground.

When he rose from prayer and went back to the disciples, he found them asleep, exhausted from sorrow.

Chapter 10

Dark Night
of the Soul

Angels Work Silently behind the Scenes

As a boy growing up, I'd often sit and stare at the painting adorning the wall of my Aunt Eula and Uncle Bob's living room. It was one artist's conception of the scene in Gethsemane that fateful Thursday evening. I still remember the angel standing ready to minister to Jesus as soon as the orders were given. Ready to wipe his brow. To ease his pain. To bandage the wounds he was about to endure. If necessary, to bring all heaven to bear on the events of this hour. Yet, no orders came. I think if you were to take a behind-the-scenes look at the situation, that artist was probably right. I think angels watched the events of this twenty-four hours with bated breath.

Gethsemane. If this scene will not bring a tear to your eye, few things will. It's a Thursday night. The next twenty-four hours will change the world forever.

The innocent Lamb of God is about to be led away

silently as a sheep before his slaughter. His soul is distressed. He knows what lies ahead. Sweat beads on his forehead. Tears well in his eyes. Words fall from his lips: "My Father, if it is possible, may this cup be taken from me. Yet not as I will, but as you will" (Matthew 26:39).

The Angels' Silence

This Scripture seems to concur with Max Lucado's assessment that during this particular twenty-four hours, the angels are amazingly silent. Only Dr. Luke refers ever so briefly to angel presence: "An angel from heaven appeared to him and strengthened him" (Luke 22:43). At a time when we think angels should jump in and save the day, they seem nowhere to be found.

The plot is complicated further by the revelation from Jesus that this is a planned absence. When Peter draws his sword to decapitate the high priest's servant, getting only an ear in the process, Jesus admonishes Peter with these words: "Do you think I cannot call on my Father, and he will at once put at my disposal more than twelve legions of angels? But how then would the Scriptures be fulfilled that say it must happen in this way?" (Matthew 26:53, 54).

"Peter, don't you know that with the snap of a finger I could have more than 72,000 angels instantaneously at my side?" The old song says, "He could have called 10,000 angels . . . but he bled and died for you and me." Perhaps for the sake of the lyric, the writer underestimates the help available, but he gets the rest right. Because of his love for you and me, Jesus' prayer that night was "not my will, but thine." This time there would be no call for the angels.

Instead, this was a time for relinquishment—a time for accepting God's will, whatever that will might be and wherever it might lead.

This was a time for trust. A time to look past the events of tomorrow to the glorious resurrection morning. Past the thorns. Past the beatings. Past the thirst. Past the wounds. Past the nails.

Maybe the doctor has just said, "Cancer." Or the boss has just said, "Fired." Or the wife has just said, "Divorce." Gethsemanes grow out of such experiences.

That's not easy to do. It's not a simple matter to look past all of that. That's why Gethsemanes are so tough. The early mystic St. John of the Cross called them "dark nights of the soul." Those agonizing, anguishing, terror-stricken nights when the darkness of loneliness closes in to suffocate you.

Maybe the doctor has just said, "Cancer." Or the boss has just said, "Fired." Or the wife has just said, "Divorce." One word can devastate you sometimes. Gethsemanes grow out of such experiences.

It's just such experiences that Bill Gaither writes about in his song "Have You Had a Gethsemane?":

> Have you prayed the night through?
> Have you shed tears of agony when hope
>   isn't in view?
> Have you prayed, "If it be Thy will, may
>   this cup pass from me,
> But if it's Thy will, oh, Lord, I will bear it
>   for Thee.[1]

God's Silence

In those moments we wonder where God is and what he's up to. He is conspicuous by his seeming absence. His silence is deafening. We want a word. An answer. An explanation.

Answers don't come. Explanations are few and far between. No one breaks the silence. Angels don't seem to arrive.

At such moments it's important to remind ourselves that because Jesus had *his* Gethsemane, *our* dark nights become more bearable, whether we realize it or not.

• We'll never experience anything that he doesn't understand—loneliness, anguish, doubts, fears—he knew them all.

• He loves us so much that he refused the impulse to call for angelic deliverance.

• He establishes the model for surrendering to the will of God.

• The empty tomb and his resurrection confirm that his choice to surrender was right: God is faithful, and life and hope await us, even if we must go through our self-made hell between here and there.

We have someone who loves, cares, and understands, even when we can't *see* the angels at work.

I'm convinced that at just such times, as in the painting on my Aunt Eula's wall, the angels are, in fact, there. They are simply silent. We may not understand why. We may wish they'd swoop down and rescue us or just hold our hand. But, they don't.

We must trust at such moments that all heaven knows that lessons in relinquishment are more important to our character than deliverance from catastrophe is to our person. Such trust does not come without Gethsemane-like sweat and tears. And if it's true of Jesus, it will most certainly be true of us.

Less than twenty-four hours after Gethsemane, Jesus shouted, "My God, my God, why have you forsaken me?" *Jesus asked why?* I guess if he can do it, I shouldn't feel guilty that I have my "why times," too.

Yet, undergirding him through the "why times" was the solid trust of "not my will, but thine,"— "Father, into thy hands I commit my spirit!" When Jesus didn't understand why, he did always know *who* was faithfully with him through it all. The God who was with Daniel in the den of lions, with Shadrach, Meshach, and Abednego through their fiery trial, and with Job through his misery, was present with his Son through Gethsemane and Calvary.

Dark Night Angels

So it is with us. He is here, even when it feels like he isn't.

Two good friends of mine share chilling stories of God's presence during what might have been disastrously dark nights in their lives:

Charlotte Greeson is a talented vocal musician and choral director. Reared in a Christian family, Charlotte is a spiritual woman and in tune with God's leading. She tells this story about an angel who came to her one dark night:

> One Friday night I was driving from Lubbock to my parents' home in Sulphur, Oklahoma, after just completing graduate school at Texas Tech University in Lubbock. I was alone, going across the caprock, when a terrible spring storm came up.
>
> I was thirty miles from the nearest town, and it was pitch black. The further I drove, the wilder the storm became. I was struggling against the

wind to keep the car between the lines of the road. Lightening flashed in my eyes, and thunder literally caused my car to shudder. Driving rain was hitting the car in huge waves. The noise was deafening, and I could hardly see ten feet in front of the car.

Needless to say, I became frightened. I was afraid to go on and too afraid to stop. So, naturally, I began to pray: "God, please protect me from this storm. Just let me get home safely, Lord. Help me to know you are near, and give me peace."

As I prayed, I became aware of a hand touching my left shoulder. It was so real that I turned my head to see who was there. Now, being alone, you'd think a hand out of the darkness would be terrifying, but this one wasn't. In fact, an amazing feeling of calm and peace slowly washed over me like a warm shower. And I knew that I was going to be fine. God was protecting me.

I drove the rest of the way home through the rain singing and unafraid. In over twenty years I've never forgotten the feeling of that hand on my shoulder. And I know I'll never forget the calmness that came with the touch of what I now believe to have been the hand of an angel in the dark night.

You met my friend Mary Hollingsworth in an earlier chapter. She tells another amazing story about a dark night and an angel:

About 1979 I was on my way from Monroe to Slidell, Louisiana, to work in a Campaign for Christ. I left after work on Friday to make the six-hour drive so I could be there for Saturday's door knocking.

If you've ever traveled the two-lane highways of inner Louisiana, you know there's no blacker night anywhere. Spanish moss hangs from the overlapping cypress trees, creating a road canopy that hides any light coming from the moon and stars. The narrow roads have no shoulders, and alligator swamps parallel the highways on both sides. There's no room for error in driving. There's no place at all for dozing off.

Besides that, in Louisiana cattle are king. They are allowed to roam freely across what they call "open range," which includes the highways, and you never know when you'll run upon a herd of them bedded down in the middle of the road.

About ten o'clock, and at sixty miles per hour, the lights on my car suddenly blinked twice and went out. An electrical problem. I came to a screeching halt for fear of plunging off into the bayou, and I sat there trying to figure out what to do. At first, I used a flashlight I had in the glove compartment to inch my way down the highway, expecting to be rammed from behind at any moment by an unsuspecting car that could not see me. After just a few minutes of that horrifying experience, I stopped again and pulled as close to the roadside as I could. What to do?

Suddenly, I saw the lights of an 18-wheel truck coming from a side road not thirty feet in front of me. The truck pulled onto the highway, headed in the same direction I was going. Then, for some unknown reason, the truck hesitated. I decided it was now or never for getting out of the swamp, and I pulled up right behind the truck. Immediately, the truck took off at breakneck speed, flying down the "cowtrail" toward the next little town, which was a good twenty-five miles away. I glued myself behind him, following closely in the multicolored lights that outlined the back of the truck. Actually, I was amazed at how well I could see in his wake.

Still petrified at the situation, I held the steering wheel in a death grip and sat on the front edge of the driver's seat like a stone statue, watching for any flicker that the truck was slowing down. One false move and my car would become a permanent part of the truck's rear axle.

When I was sure I could not go another mile, we pulled into a dark, tiny town that had obviously rolled up its sidewalks hours before. The truck began to slow down, and finally came to a stop in front of an old filling station. What a surprise to find that it was still open.

I breathed a giant sigh of relief and got out of the car. I walked into the station to find a friendly old man. I said, "Just a minute; I'll be right back." And I walked outside to thank the truck driver. No more than a few seconds had passed. The truck was gone. Just gone. I didn't hear the truck drive away, even though its engine was loud. I didn't see the lights fading into the distance, even though there's no way the truck had had time to get out of sight. It had just disappeared, plain and simple. And, even more strangely, the old man in the station never saw the huge truck at all. He only heard and saw my car drive up.

Frankly, I haven't told this story very often through the years. My Christian friends tend to look at me with that critical you're-a-little-weird look that makes you feel like you've lost a few marbles. And telling them that an angel driving an 18-wheeler rescued you is pretty risky. They file you away under "Caution: Loose Screw" and whisper to each other behind your back.

In truth, I'm convinced it was an angel of God that came out of nowhere at precisely the right moment to lead me safely through the swamp, the alligators, the cattle, and the black of night to a tiny dimly lit filling station where I could get help. And you can think I'm crazy or weird or one brick short of a load if you want to. But I was there. It happened to me. I'll never discount God's faithful protection or cease to give him the praise.

The darkest of nights in our lives are blackened—not by the hour on the clock, but by the circumstances we encounter. The dark nights of the soul—those are the darkest nights of all.

In October, 1993, exactly one year after the death of my dad, I received a call that the second most influential adult male in my life was about to die at his home. Joan and I immediately drove to Uncle Bob's house.

We arrived less than fifteen minutes before his death, just long enough for me to spend some time alone with him. As I stroked his hand and assured him that it was all right to let go, I recalled that bright spring Sunday morning years earlier when this man I loved and respected had walked the aisle of our church to ask me to baptize him.

In those last moments of his life, our eyes met as his glassy stare pierced my heart. He took his final breath, and went home.

As I walked into the living room to tell Aunt Eula

that Bob had gone, I glanced above her head to see the picture of Jesus in Gethsemane that had so mesmerized me as a child. The angel was still there just as he'd been years earlier. Waiting.

I thought to myself, "The angels are here right now. They are most certainly here." For Jesus there were times when the angels didn't seem to come. They weren't even called. Could have been. Weren't.

Gethsemanes are no picnic.
The toughest times to walk hand in
hand with heaven are
when the angels are silent.

For us, there may be similar times—times that we'll see in retrospect as the most productive periods of spiritual growth in our lives. When such times occur, they hurt. Gethsemanes are no picnic. The toughest times to walk hand in hand with heaven are when the angels are silent. When your own Gethsemane arrives, remember that while the angels may be silent, they are most definitely present, working behind the scenes to carry us through the dark nights of the soul. Praise God for his faithfulness!

Notes

[1]"Have You Had a Gethsemane?" Words and music by William J. Gaither. © 1963 William J. Gaither. All rights reserved. Used by permission.

Focusing Your Faith:

1. Imagine you were there with Jesus in the garden of Gethsemane (Matthew 26). What would you consider the most memorable part of that night?

2. If you had overheard Jesus' prayer, what would have been your reaction? Why?

3. Jesus gave up his right to call for angelic deliverance in order to fulfill Scripture. For whose benefit was this sacrifice made? Why?

4. How do you feel knowing that accepting God's will may require suffering through your own dark nights?

5. What promises of God can you rely on to strengthen your faith during these times? How can angels help you?

6. How has a personal "dark night of the soul" experience helped you grow spiritually?

7. Pray now for the Lord to empower you with the trust necessary to face your next Gethsemane.

Acts 27:23-25

Last night an angel of the God whose I am and whom I serve stood beside me and said, "Do not be afraid, Paul. You must stand trial before Caesar; and God has graciously given you the lives of all who sail with you." So keep up your courage, men, for I have faith in God that it will happen just as he told me.

Chapter 11

God
Hasn't Changed

Angels Carry Out God's Will Today

Y ou may have heard the story of the priest who lived in a monastery where the vow of silence demanded that a person speak only two words every six years. At the end of his first six years of silence this priest uttered the words: "Bed hard."

Twelve years brought the words: "Room hot."

At eighteen years, he said, "Food bad!"

Finally after twenty-four years, he exclaimed, "I quit!"

His superior immediately replied, "I'm not surprised. For almost a quarter of a century, all you've done is gripe, gripe, gripe!"

A case can be made for silence. Our world is awfully noisy at times. Blaring stereos. Roaring televisions. Purring computers. No wonder we seem to have such a difficult time hearing the "voice" of God. We're strangers to the very silence necessary for such a task.

One thing that jumps off the page as the Book of Acts chronicles the life of the early church is the early Christians' amazing capacity to detect the behind-the-scenes involvement of God in their lives. Also impressive is their willingness to respond obediently to God's promptings. Perhaps these are facets of New Testament Christianity we'd do well to consider getting really serious about restoring.

I promised you that we would be talking mostly about what angels *do*—not what angels *did*. I hope you've been blessed by the practical, present-day applications and testimonials from sane, credible, reliable Christians who are convinced that they have experienced the interaction of heaven and earth.

I think it's important to approach the topic of angels in this way. First of all, angels do not fit into our handy little hermeneutical, predispensed packages. For example, we might conclude that some things were for the Old Testament dispensation only and, therefore, were ushered out at Calvary by being "nailed to the cross." However, that rule doesn't apply to angels. They are every bit as active in the life of the early church in the Book of Acts as they were in the Old Testament. No wonder the Hebrews writer observes: "Isn't it obvious that all angels are sent to help out with those lined up to receive salvation? (Hebrews 1:14, TM).

At other times, we latch onto a verse in the New Testament that "proves"—or so we conclude—that certain things were reserved only for the first century. When the New Testament was completed, the reasoning goes, such things were no longer necessary. Most of the things that fall into this category involve supernatural gifts employed by human beings. Trying to apply any of these passages to angelic activity presents some serious theological problems.

Since angels are God's emissaries to do his work, concluding that their activity ceased at the end of the first century would be to conclude that God's activity ceased at the end of the first century. That would be heresy of the first magnitude. Such a conclusion would make us deists—we would be saying that God got all of this started and then stepped back out of the picture and left the rest to us in our puny power. I don't know about you, but I don't buy that option.

> *Let's stop being afraid*
> *to celebrate the dynamic*
> *activity of God in our lives.*

So the biblical doctrine of angels is good for us. It keeps us thinking and stretching. It reminds us that God cannot be boxed up or figured out. Mystery, adventure, and surprise become a part of each day as we await what God might be doing among us today. We can spend our lives playing word games about whether angel activity should be appropriately labeled miracle or providence, but we find it difficult to deny that our God is alive, well, and actively involved in the lives of his children. Rather than debate dogmatics, I choose to enjoy the ride and praise God for anything and everything he decides to do in my life. With him every day is lived in the supernatural. Let's stop being afraid to celebrate the dynamic activity of God in our lives.

Celebrate!

Whenever I think of celebrating God's active

presence here, I recall a significant incident at one of the first churches I worked for nearly thirty years ago. One of our older, highly respected, and dearly loved members had been diagnosed with a massive lung tumor.

Since he was scheduled for surgery on Thursday morning, our little church gathered early on Wednesday evening for a concentrated prayer time in which we begged God to spare this good man's life.

When the doctors left the operating room the next morning, they announced to the family that apparently "some mistake had been made"—no tumor was found in his lung.

The thing that amazes me the most about this is how *little* we made of the incident after the fact. Oh, we were thankful—kinda, sorta. Yet, it's as if we were afraid to say much for fear that to honor God too much in such a situation might raise questions we could not answer. Questions like, Why would God heal him and not this other fellow?

So we blushed. We stammered. We stuttered. We were glad a "mistake had been made." And almost apologetically, we said a slight thanks that God had "answered our prayer."

What I'm saying is that I don't believe God "answered" (blush) our prayer. I believe that God ANSWERED (celebrate!) our prayer. I think the only "mistake" made during this process was our failure to give God all the praise, honor, and glory he deserves for each powerful activity in our lives.

I'm not talking about some glitzy, dazzling sideshow healing service. I'm talking about God's people *believing* that God still sends his angels to answer the heartfelt prayers they lift to him. I, for one, believe he does.

Why Not Me?

I know that scores of tough questions arise when a discussion turns to God's answering prayer.

"If an angel helped that person in this way, why didn't he help me in my plight?" One reason we ask that is because we don't have the privilege of seeing the big picture. We forget at times that God's wise sovereignty is better than we might imagine.

There's a story in ancient lore of an angel and a prophet who go from ship to ship trying to get passage, only to be refused. Finally, a kind gentleman welcomes them aboard his new, shiny ship. As they reach the other side, the angel punctures the side of the new boat. The prophet asks, "Why are you treating this kind man in such a horrible way? You're destroying his new boat!" Later, the prophet discovers that the next day _every_ functional boat and its captain were sent out to war where the men died in battle. Because this man's boat was punctured, his life was spared.

The ancients used this story to teach their children that we do not always see things as they actually are. Things that appear to be horrific losses are often, in the long run, tremendous victories for all involved. So the fact that an angel has _not_ rescued me may actually be the greatest blessing of all.

Why Me?

The operative question should not be, Why not me? The real question should be, Why me? asked by the person who has received amazing blessings. There lies the _real_ issue: Why was _my_ life spared? Why was _my_ illness cured? What purpose does God have for _my_ being here? There must be a reason.

If we dodge all the tough questions, our faith will

become withered, pale, and anemic. Only by committing our lives to God-reality—even without having all the answers—will we experience life at its best. If we could gain a we're-all-here-for-a-purpose mentality, our faith and our spiritual productivity would be more in line with God's wishes and ways.

Angels in Acts

Nowhere is vibrant, radiant faith more vividly apparent than in the life of the early church. In the Book of Acts, angels appear everywhere.

In Acts 5, the apostles are jailed because they stubbornly refuse to stop preaching about Jesus. The miracles they perform are becoming a source of consternation to the jealous Sadducees, who do not believe in miracles or angels or the resurrection (23:8). In a moment of irony, God sends an angel to deliver his apostles out of prison.

Isn't that just like our God? I can't help but smile when I think of the sea of surprised faces on judgment day who'll be shouting, "But you can't do that!" We'd better let God be God.

Take the end-times controversy, for example. Somebody has to be upset on judgment day over that topic. Premillennialists? Amillennialists? Postmillennialists? I don't know exactly who's going to be upset, but somebody's bound to be shouting, "God, you can't do it that way!" Each doctrinal position has God boxed up so that he can't possibly choose to bring the world to an end in any way other than what their preaching prescribes. Well, hold on, because our God is a God of surprises.

The Calvin family developed our eschatology (theology of the end times) years ago. Basically it goes like this: Any way God chooses to bring the world to an end and take us to heaven, we'll let him do it. He's the Boss. End of discussion. Does that sound too simplistic? All I know is, while the Sadducees were down at the local synagogue preaching a sermon called "There're No Such Things as Angels," an angel was releasing the apostles from jail. I'm willing to let God be God.

Chapters 8 and 10 of Acts share inspiring accounts of angel activity regarding the preaching of the gospel. In Acts 8, an angel approaches Philip and points him in the direction of a seeker, a eunuch from Ethiopia. The timing is perfect. What a marvelous moment when the eunuch connects the prophecies of the Messiah to Jesus of Nazareth, and the eunuch insists upon stopping the chariot and being baptized then and there.

In chapter 10, it is a Gentile seeker named Cornelius. An angel in shining clothes tells him exactly what steps to take to discover the good news of Jesus Christ. Cornelius bursts the bubble of those who try to prove that prayer is reserved only for a select few who have undergone the appropriate initiation rites to present themselves worthy of prayer. Again, God is full of surprises.

In Acts 8, the evangelist is visited by the angel and told to approach the seeker. In Acts 10, the seeker is approached by the angel and told to send for the apostle. I think sometimes God does things differently from case to case in Acts just to keep us on our toes and to help us avoid the temptation to box him up into our personal prepackaged pattern.

Angels are at work again in Acts 12. Herod is on the loose. He has already killed James, and Peter is next. God hears the prayers of the disciples and sends an angel to deliver Peter from prison, which, strangely enough, amazes Peter and astounds those praying for his release. Herod starts thinking himself God. But Jehovah will not be mocked. When the prideful king takes credit for being God, the angel of the Lord strikes Herod, and he "was eaten by worms and died." So much for his self-proclaimed deity.

One of the most poignant and powerful pictures of angel activity is in Acts 27. A storm is raging. Things look hopeless for Paul and Luke. After everything humanly possible has been done, God intervenes. Listen to Paul's testimony:

> Last night an angel of the God whose I am and whom I serve stood beside me and said, "Do not be afraid, Paul. You must stand trial before Caesar; and God has graciously given you the lives of all who sail with you." So keep up your courage, men, for I have faith in God that it will happen just as he told me (vv. 23-25).

What a powerful passage! So typical of our God. When we're at the end of our rope, God is there. When things look impossible, with him it is possible. And, when all appears hopeless, with him there is hope. As is typical throughout Scripture, it is an angel who brings the word of comfort—"Don't be afraid." No fear!

Entertaining Angels

Not only is there no "proof text" that suggests angel activity has stopped, there is, in fact, one verse that suggests it hasn't. Hebrews 13:2 states: "Do not forget to entertain strangers, for by so doing some people have entertained angels without knowing it." While the obvious topic of this verse is Christian hospitality, the motivation is the possibility of serving angels.

This picture reminds me of Jesus' parable in

which the king shocks his court by saying,

> For I was hungry and you gave me something to
> eat, I was thirsty and you gave me something to
> drink, I was a stranger and you invited me in, I
> needed clothes and you clothed me, I was sick
> and you looked after me, I was in prison and you
> came to visit me (Matthew 25:35, 36).

To this the righteous answer, "Lord, when . . . ?"
They then repeat his list of deeds, not remembering
doing such things for the king. Then comes the
king's reply: "I tell you the truth, whatever you did
for one of the least of these brothers of mine, you did
for me" (v. 40).

In one sense, we never know whom we're helping, do we? In another sense, we always know whom
we're helping: God.

What a note of anticipation the "entertaining
angels without knowing it" passage breathes into
each day of our lives. What a difference it would
make in our interpersonal relationships if we were
to treat everyone we encounter on any given day as
if they were angels from God.

The waitress would faint if we gave her an angel-
sized tip. The barber would be shocked if we listened
to him with as much interest as if he were an angel.
The boy that carries our groceries to the car each
week would be delighted if we were as interested in
his life, his dreams, as we would be were he an angel.

Would we manipulate that customer if we knew
she was an angel? Would we overcharge that client if
we guessed she might be walking out our door right
back into heaven's hallways? Would we snap at our
wife if she were an angel? Would we scream at our
kids if we knew they have a direct line to heaven?

Things would change, wouldn't they, if we really

believed Hebrews 13:2. Our marriages would be
better, our business would be conducted differently,
our casual acquaintances would take on a more
positive flavor.

You might be saying, "But you don't understand.
I *know* all these folks you mentioned, and they're no
angels—believe me." To that I say, "I wouldn't be too
sure." You see, what isn't covered by the Hebrews 13
"angels without knowing it" umbrella, is covered by
the Matthew 25 "least of these" umbrella.

Both passages attempt to open our eyes as Christians to the sacred opportunities that are ours each
day. Both passages try to stifle our pretentious ten-
dency to divide the sacred and the secular. Both
passages display the thin veil that exists between
time and eternity. Both passages open our eyes to the
supernatural all around us. Both passages say, "Treat
folks right because there's a spark of the divine in
each person you meet." You've never met a person
who is unimportant to God. And you never will.

> *I wake up each morning realizing*
> *that I might encounter a legitimate,*
> *true-blue, bona fide angel today.*

I don't want to "water down" the Hebrews 13
passage. I believe it means what it says and says
what it means. I wake up each morning realizing
that I might encounter a legitimate, true-blue, bona
fide angel today. That makes every day an adventure. Getting up is easy when you're facing that kind
of day. Words like *dull, boring*, and *humdrum*
should be foreign to the Christian's vocabulary. So
the next time you get a strong impression to do some

kindness for someone, remember my wife's acronym: **J**ust **O**bey **A**ll **N**udges. That's a pretty good philosophy to live by.

Our God is alive and active. He is involved with our lives on a daily basis. And the next person you meet just might be one of his angels. Don't ever forget that! After all, we are walking hand in hand with heaven.

In an earlier chapter you met our neighbors Wade and Emma Felps. Their daughter Jenni New shares a story which shows her dad's openness to God's nudgings.

> Several months ago my dad went through a serious health crisis. During those days of lying in the hospital, Dad recalls that he became deeply convicted that he needed to tell the people closest to him how much they mean to him. He felt that he'd not told Emma's parents prior to their death, and he didn't want to make the same mistake with others.

> Recently, my mom attended a family reunion with her sisters, making a three-hour drive from our home. Was she surprised when she saw Dad walk into the gathering! He'd driven all the way so he could sit down with her sisters and tell each one personally how they had blessed his life. Upon finishing, he drove back home, leaving them to continue their reunion.

> My aunts have since said that Dad's words were some of the most encouraging and affirming of their lives, all because my dad chose to be responsive to the strong impressions which God brought into his life.

> To show that such obedience to divine promptings

can cross generations, listen to Jenni's own story concerning an unexplainable urge she had one day to go to the park.

> One day, I got a strong urge to spend the day in the park with my kids. The urge was so strong that the "better offers" that came along were all rejected—which, in itself, was unusual for me.
>
> I was sitting in the park, enjoying my kids, yet wondering why in the world I was there when other places would have provided equally good family time. At that moment, I recognized a Christian sister sitting on a bench across the park.
>
> Knowing that she was facing a serious cancer surgery in a few days, I approached her to see how she was doing. She told me that she was feeling really "down" that day and had been prompted to bring her granddaughter to the park to escape the depression of staying at home.
>
> I told her about my not knowing exactly why I was there that day. After our heartfelt prayer together, she looked into my eyes and, through the tears, said, "I know why you're here today. God sent you here to pray with me. I feel so much better knowing that I'm not facing this cancer alone."
>
> I'll always be glad I obeyed the impulse to go to the park that day. My life was changed forever.

God's church is comprised of people—ordinary people, but servants of an extraordinary God. God's angels stand side by side with us, nudging us to do his will. When we cooperate with their nudgings, they can produce some amazing results!

Focusing Your Faith:

1. Do you think the people in the early church were as shocked to see an angel as you would be?

2. Review Acts 27:23-25: If you'd been aboard Paul's ship and heard his angel testimony, would you have believed him? Why?

3. Do you think our reluctance to believe in the spirit world might diminish angelic appearances? Why?

4. Why do you think God continues to send his special messengers to assist those who don't believe angels exist? Would you?

5. Missionaries tell us that many world cultures are much more accepting of angelic appearance testimonies. To what do you attribute their openness?

6. Name a circumstance or situation in which you'd love more than anything for an angel to appear and offer advice or assistance.

7. Since God is Spirit, pray to be more open, accepting, and expectant of his supernatural activity.

Ephesians 6:10-18

Finally, be strong in the Lord and in his mighty power. Put on the full armor of God so that you can take your stand against the devil's schemes. For our struggle is not against flesh and blood, but against the rulers, against the authorities, against the powers of this dark world and against the spiritual forces of evil in the heavenly realms. Therefore put on the full armor of God, so that when the day of evil comes, you may be able to stand your ground, and after you have done everything, to stand. Stand firm then, with the belt of truth buckled around your waist, with the breastplate of righteousness in place, and with your feet fitted with the readiness that comes from the gospel of peace. In addition to all this, take up the shield of faith, with which you can extinguish all the flaming arrows of the evil one. Take the helmet of salvation and the sword of the Spirit, which is the word of God. And pray in the Spirit on all occasions with all kinds of prayers and requests. With this in mind, be alert and always keep on praying for all the saints.

Chapter 12

There's a
War Going On!

Angels Fight Satanic Forces

I'll never forget one particular counseling case. Its implications still reverberate in my mind. Hundreds of marital problems come before me annually. Each of them testifies to the presence of sin in our world. Each reminds me that Satan wants to destroy the Christian home. Yet never in my practice have I been so convinced that an all-out attack was being launched from Satan and his powers in the unseen realm as I was in this case. Unbridled spiritual warfare was being unleashed behind the scenes. Satanic cultic activity. Incest. Perversions of the most despicable sort. The signs were too obvious to miss. This couple was engaged in spiritual warfare. And at the time they came to me, Satan was winning the battle.

Since the publication of Frank Peretti's book *This Present Darkness*, the interest level among Christians to know more about the spiritual warfare which occurs in the unseen realm has run high. Joe Beam's recent book, *Seeing the Unseen,* and his audio cassette tapes, *Spiritual Warfare,* address the entire spectrum of the spiritual domain.

I have chosen to make the focus of this volume our allies in the cosmic struggle—God's angels who are aligned on our side and continually work on our behalf. I realize, however, that we might cultivate a greater appreciation of the angels working *for* us if we better understood the forces arrayed *against* us. Therefore, this chapter will briefly summarize what others have devoted entire volumes to.

The Masked Marauder

Satan began as an angel of God, a magnificent cherub, a guardian of the Garden of Eden (Ezekiel 28:12-17). So what went wrong? How could God's splendid creation turn into the source of evil? *I,* too, am God's splendid creation—an example of something good that went bad. And so are you. We all sin and fall short of the glory of God. That double-edged sword called *choice* did that to us. I think it did it to Satan, too. Satan rebelled and fell from the ranks of heaven, and his pride and self-centeredness leaves him incapable of responding to redemption.

I don't get my theology from Milton or Dante, although I think they may have been better theologians than we give them credit for. I believe as I do about Satan because it's the only explanation to be derived anywhere from Scripture that makes sense to me.

Satan is *not* a mere presence of an uncreated, eternal evil. In the Book of Job, Satan asks God's permission to attack Job and rob him of all of his earthly treasures, which Satan believes are the only things holding Job to God.

That tells us two things. First of all, it tells us that Satan is not God's equal. God is in charge. No matter how powerful Satan may seem, we can still cling to this knowledge: "greater is he that is in you, than he that is in the world" (1 John 4:4, KJV).

The Job story also tells us that Satan doesn't hold us in very high regard. He assumes we are like him—selfish, manipulative, greedy—that our only tie with God is for the rewards that go along with the package. Perhaps there have been those throughout history who've lived down to Satan's expectations by denying God and becoming cynically embittered at the first hint of trouble or loss, but Job is not one of them. God expects the best from Job— that Job is in it for the relationship, not the re- wards—and Job proves God right.

Throughout Scripture we discover that Satan's beauty disintegrates into self-love, his intellect gives way to arrogance, and his wealth becomes greed. He is crafty, sneaky, deceptive. He lies at the drop of a hat. He is aggressive, not passive, stalking us like a hungry lion.

Satan wears whatever mask he needs in order to deceive us. He'll parade himself as "an angel of light" (2 Corinthians 11:14) if that will help him reach his goals. He'll even stoop to telling the truth if neces- sary. For example, he'll gladly remind us that we're sinners. That's the truth—we are. What he won't choose to tell us is the other side of the story.

According to tradition, someone approached Martin Luther on one occasion with a list of what they perceived to be his transgressions. Luther sent him away to think of more. Upon his return with a more complete list, Martin Luther remarked, "Now, write across the page in bold red letters: 'Debt Paid in Full by Jesus Christ!' " That is the truth that the devil won't tell us.

There's a War Going On

Not only is Satan, the masked marauder, personally on the prowl to destroy us, he has, in fact, a massive military build-up in the unseen realm with an arsenal of artillery aimed in our direction. Scripture is explicit in its teaching that our wrestlings are not against flesh and blood but against principalities and powers in the heavenly realm (Ephesians 6).

Angels, good and bad, are highly organized into a hierarchical structure par excellence. There are archangels, angels, seraphim, and cherubim. Certain angels are assigned as princes of various nations (Daniel 10). And throughout the apocalyptic portions of Scripture, including John's Revelation, a continual invisible battle rages between the forces of good and the forces of evil.

Something as seemingly insignificant as the birth of a baby boy in Bethlehem causes clashes in the heavenlies of cosmic proportions. And the aftershock of six hours one Friday afternoon outside Jerusalem still reverberates through the corridors of the unseen realm. Such passages as Daniel 10 indicate that great lengthy battles rage over the fate of nations. And Peter's allusion to what Jesus went through between the crucifixion and the resurrection indicates that all heaven broke loose to defeat the hell which had bound us (1 Peter 3:18-20).

Scripture indicates that as massive as these military operations are, they are mounting toward an ultimate cosmic clash so unbelievable in proportions that the world as we know it will not survive. Yet, God has already revealed to us the outcome of this battle: Lord Jesus will ride in on his white horse and carry the redeemed home. With Jesus, even losers win. Because he has already won, we cannot lose. What a powerful promise!

We Are Not the Enemy

One practical reason for understanding Satan and his strategy is so that we'll be able to recognize and admit to ourselves and each other who the real enemy is.

Sometimes we treat each other as though we were the enemy. We scream at the wife. We yell at the kids. We attack a brother in Christ through lecture or publication. I'm certain that Satan does handsprings over such behaviors. For as long as he can keep us fussing at each other, he has a free reign of terror in our lives.

We are not the enemy! Satan is. What a difference it would make in our treatment of others if we understood that. If the wife whose husband left her for his secretary could direct her anger at the real culprit, Satan, what a difference it would make in her life. Her husband might be so shocked at her response to him that she might even win him back. We must stop getting mad at the wrong people. If we directed nearly as much mental and emotional energy at Satan as we do at "straw men" we erect as enemies, we'd be making giant strides in spiritual growth.

A Personal Inventory

Can we be honest enough with ourselves to take a personal inventory, which could perhaps reveal how successfully Satan is being allowed to make inroads into our lives? Ask yourself these questions:

1. How often does pride get in my way and

prompt me to do things I shouldn't (like go along with the crowd) or prevent me from doing things I should (like saying an honest "I'm sorry")?

2. How frequently does selfishness motivate my behavior?

3. Do I tend to judge others on the basis of their outward beauty, wealth, or intellect?

4. Are any or all of these factors—beauty, wealth, or intellect—driving forces in my view of myself?

5. Do I feel often that it's my place to shake my fist at God and demand that he treat me better? After all, I have my rights.

6. Do I, at times, fill the role of being accuser of God, myself, or others?

7. Have I spent enough time with Jesus lately to recognize the obvious absence of these first six things in his life?

If my honest answers to these questions indicate that I'm losing the battle, then I need to focus my attention upon developing the spiritual armor described in Ephesians 6. As was Jesus, I need to become more and more conversant with the Word of God. Jesus employed Scripture to defeat Satan. So must we.

We need to daily deepen our walk with Jesus through Bible study and prayer. Spiritual disciplines must come first in our lives.

The Victory Is Ours

There's a war going on, brothers and sisters. And we need to be armed for battle. Thank God his angels are in the fray with us. Yet, don't let that knowledge be an excuse for not preparing to participate in the victory which is already ours.

Often in the heat of the battle we must be reminded of the simple truths about God. Barbara New, wife of Sweet Publishing chairman, Bill New, tells the following story of how God taught her and Bill about God's desire to be our God of Provision, Jehovah Jireh:

> When my husband, Bill, was suddenly taken ill with a severe stroke in November 1993, the days and weeks in intensive care grew increasingly stressful. I could see him for only a few minutes, a few times a day.
>
> His life hung in the balance, and he faced total, or at best, partial paralysis—if he lived. We were sustained by prayers sent up by people everywhere. We received more strength from those prayers than I could have ever imagined.
>
> One particular evening at the hospital, Satan was working overtime on my fears. Someone from the hospital office came to tell me that there was a problem with our insurance—they might not pay. Someone else advised me to make sure I had "power of attorney" in the event of Bill's total disability—or it would be impossible to operate our business. I was almost overcome with fear.
>
> That night I was too exhaused to sleep—so stressed from concern for Bill and dread of the unknown. I thought if I could just go out into the night and look up at the stars as Abraham had done that I would somehow feel close to God, and I would know his promises to me also were valid.
>
> About 4:00 A.M. I went out into my backyard to

see an overcast sky. Not one star was visible anywhere, but God's presence was there. He spoke—not audibly, but into my heart: "Just because you cannot see the stars, does not mean they are not shining. TRUST IN ME!"

I was comforted knowing I must see with the eyes of faith. I went back into the house, and he showed me Psalm 27:14: "Wait for the Lord—be strong—take heart—and WAIT FOR THE LORD."

I remember that peace engulfed my whole being, and I was able to drift off to sleep for a few hours. I knew that no matter what happened, God would provide.

Bill is still recuperating. But God has blessed him with a remarkable recovery. He's been through months of therapy. Sometimes the process has seemed slow, but we are so thankful. He does have some disabilities—but much less than we feared. God has truly been our provision!

We are both still waiting on the Lord. God has led us to begin a weekly prayer group in our home for the sick, the lame, and the hurting. What a blessing! We never know whom God will bring to our door. There have been many. God has healed some, and some he has not.

We are learning to praise and pray and wait. He provides for us day by day, step by step, as we learn to always look only to him for what we need.

The war goes on, every day, every hour, in every heart and life. God's angels line up on our side; Satan's angels line up on the other side. The battle is for our souls. Thank God that his angels are beside us, and the war has already been won in Christ alone.

Focusing Your Faith:

1. The Bible tells us that Satan is a deceiver, an imposter, a roaring lion, a serpent, the ruler of demons, and the prince of darkness. How do these descriptions make you feel?

2. What is the most devastating lie Satan has worked overtime to convince you of? How did you discover it was a lie?

3. Can you think of a time when Satan appeared to you as an "angel of light" (2 Corinthians 11:14)?

4. Recall a time you felt empowered by the Holy Spirit to withstand Satan and his evil army.

5. What advice would you give a Christian friend who feels overwhelmed by Satan's forces?

6. Take inventory of your life. Where are Satan's evil forces most obviously at work?

7. Pray that God will give you the courage and strength to trust in the power of the Holy Spirit to defeat Satanic strongholds in your life.

Revelation 4:11

You are worthy, our Lord and God,
    to receive glory and honor and power,
for you created all things,
    and by your will they were created
    and have their being.

Chapter 13

Home Free!

Angels Complete the Mission

I love the song "Home Free!" by contemporary Christian artist Wayne Watson. In the song's stanzas he chronicles the faith struggles which grow out of life's difficult days. But what I love best about the song is its chorus which recalls for us in an encouraging refrain that one of these days the problems will end, and we'll be "home free." I like that. I think it's the truth.

These words have become especially meaningful to a good friend of mine who prefers to remain unnamed. She tells this story of her husband's death:

> My husband and I have been best friends for as long as I can remember. That's what made all of this so hard. It's all happened so fast.
>
> Just weeks ago he went into the hospital for what was to be routine surgery. How wrong you can be assuming that everything will go smoothly and life will return to normal in a snap. Not so.

Words cannot express the shock we felt as the doctors announced to us that my husband had an advanced form of cancer which would claim his life in a matter of weeks. Only those who've heard such words can understand the feeling they bring. No one else can come close to understanding.

Neither can anyone who's not been through it understand the sheer exhaustion which envelopes you—physically and emotionally—during the days and weeks following such an announcement. Your life becomes a frantic whiz of activity—trying frantically to do something—anything—which might prolong life a bit. Yet, at the same time, you're trying to grab every moment and make it special, because you know there aren't too many of those moments left.

It's one of the most trying experiences of life to see someone you dearly love wasting away before your eyes. To see vigor and strength replaced by weakness and dependence. It tears at your heart.

Then came those all-too-special moments at the end. I thank God daily for those. All that could be done medically had been done. Although the pain was excruciating, my husband refused the morphine they offered because he wanted to be coherent to the end.

We talked of our life together—our wedding twenty-five years ago. The births of our three children. He shared his concerns about mine and the kids' future. He made certain that all was in order.

We spoke of spiritual things with a depth unknown to us in times past. Then he dozed off into a sleep from which I thought he'd never awaken.

I was wrong. On the last morning of his life, he aroused and awoke. He told me he loved me. He asked to see the kids. He looked us all in the eyes, and with a big smile on his face he said, "I'm going to be all right. I know because I saw the angels. Don't you worry about me. I love you. Just remember—I saw the angels . . . the angels."

He closed his eyes for the last time.

Had you known my husband you would appreciate the majesty of those moments. He was a wonderful man who loved God dearly. But he was a left-brained, computer-genius accountant who had no use for "fanatics" in religious circles who go around telling everyone about their subjective, emotional experiences. Angels were definitely _not_ his style.

I believe with all my heart—and always will—that my husband _did_ see the angels and returned momentarily to encourage us with his discovery. I thank God for allowing that to occur!

Oh, I've still gone through grief. It's been tough. I lost my best friend. But knowing that the angels took my husband into the arms of his best friend, Jesus, has made the adjustment so much easier to make. Through this all, Jesus has become my best friend, too.

Angels are on a mission. One of their most important jobs is protecting and encouraging God's people. That keeps them pretty busy. They're in and out of heaven a lot.

One of these days, though, their mission will be complete. Job over. Finished. They'll be called home for good—never to have to go out on another mission again. Then they can spend all their time at the other thing they already do a lot of—gathering around the throne and praising God. What a life!

On that glorious day when God calls all his children home, the angels will accompany us. The new heaven and new earth will be ushered in, and all creatures great and small—human and angelic—will join the heavenly chorus.

---

*On that glorious day when God
calls all his children home,
the angels will accompany us.*

We'll all hear their triumphant song:

"Holy, holy, holy
is the Lord God Almighty,
who was, and is, and is to come" (Revelation 4:8).

"You are worthy, our Lord and God,
to receive glory and honor and power,
for you created all things,
and by your will they were created
and have their being" (Revelation 4:11).

Then I looked and heard the voice of many angels, numbering thousands upon thousands, and ten thousand times ten thousand. They encircled the throne and the living creatures and the elders. In a loud voice they sang:

"Worthy is the Lamb, who was slain,
to receive power and wealth and wisdom and
strength
and honor and glory and praise!"
(Revelation 5:11, 12).

"For the Lamb at the center of the throne will

be their shepherd;
he will lead them to springs of living water.
And God will wipe away every tear from their
eyes" (Revelation 7:17).

What an occasion! I can hardly wait. Can you?
It's no wonder, is it, that early Christians ended
their prayers with the phrase, "Come, Lord Jesus!"
They understood some truths that have seemingly
gotten watered down by the centuries. Maybe we
need to be reminded.

The War Is Won

Yes, there is a war going on, but Revelation was
written by aged and banished John to encourage
Christians to persevere through troubles because
Jesus is Lord—he's Boss, he's in charge. Nothing is
as out of control as it may seem to be at times.
Christians have been given the privilege of reading
the last page of history. We know how it all turns
out, and it's good. Death is not the victor. Satan is
not the master. Evil is not the winner.

Jesus wins in the end, folks. Remind yourself of
that when the way gets weary and the world seems
to be getting so wicked that it appears for certain
that evil will carry the day. Not so. Jesus is Lord!

The Victory Is Sure

Not only is the outcome of the universal struggle
between good and evil assured, so is your personal
salvation if you are a Christian. John says, "I write
these things to you who believe in the name of the
Son of God so that you may know that you have
eternal life" (1 John 5:13). To John, eternal life is not
a quantity of life that begins at death. Rather, it is a
quality of life that begins at the new birth. And John

is quite intent that we Christians *know* that this thing called life is ours in Jesus.

In the name of battling the abuses of a "once saved, always saved" theology, many of us have sacrificed our assurance of salvation. Many of us Christians live in constant fear and insecurity. Still others of us live as though it all depends on the perfection of our performance.

Christian, take heart. Praise God for Calvary! Salvation is about the victory over Satan that Jesus won when he emerged from his tomb that glorious Sunday morning.

Eternal life is not a quantity of life that begins at death. Rather, it is a quality of life that begins at the new birth.

So, Christian, celebrate! Fix your eyes on Jesus, the author and finisher of our faith. Set your mind on heaven. Store your treasures in heaven. Then wait for the homecoming.

We Are Nomads

It sounds so easy, but sometimes we get distracted—we get sidetracked. One problem that binds us to this earth is that we forget that we're all nomads—just passing through. To look at some of our material goods, you might get the impression that we plan on being here forever. Sometimes we get that impression, too. We drive our tent pegs too deeply into the ground. The lap of luxury is often the last place to develop a heavenly mindset.

Deuteronomy warns the Israelites of that very thing. God says that if they aren't careful, they'll build nice homes, set rich tables, and forget where all of it comes from. The Book of Amos tells us that's exactly what happened to Israel.

It can also happen to us.

Praise the Lord!

Heaven is our home. And someday, thanks to Jesus, we're going there. Once home, we'll join the angels, who've been our helpers through our lifetime, as we all lift a beautiful chorus of praise to God.

Will it be Stamps-Baxter or Mozart? Luther's refrains or contemporary Christian? I have no idea. My guess is that it'll be much like on the Day of Pentecost—everyone will hear in his own language. Everyone will praise in his own style.

But won't that get boring—just singing and praising forever? Two questions: (1) Have you ever attended a _really_ good praise service? I never want them to end. I vividly recall attending a Bill Gaither concert years ago where he introduced a young soloist on a tour with him for the first time. When she finished her song, a spontaneous standing ovation erupted. It was one of the most moving experiences of my life. I could have listened to her all night long. Her name was Sandi Patty. Nothing compares to the joy which explodes in mighty praise. (2) Do you ever get tired of showing pictures of your fiancé or your children or your grandkids? It never gets boring to express your love. In heaven we'll have an eternity to praise God for all he has done for us. No one who's there will ever get bored doing that. I guarantee.

Thirty years. It seems impossible. Three decades ago I accepted my first preaching position. I was a still-wet-behind-the-ears college freshman who didn't know much about anything, except that I wanted to share the message of Jesus with folks who'd listen. I've done that now for 1,500 Sundays.

In addition, Joan and I celebrate twenty-nine years of marriage this year. We're just one year away from AARP membership. Time flies.

It seems like only yesterday Joan and I stood before the Lord and took our vows of marriage.

It seems like early this morning when we walked up to the glass nursery window those three times and viewed our brand new arrivals: Jim, Laurie, and Lisa.

It seems like an hour ago we hid Easter eggs for our toddlers or burned the midnight oil assembling Christmas surprises for our preschoolers.

It seems like fifteen minutes ago we attended high school graduation for our now-adult children.

It seems like five minutes ago we went to the college graduation of our two oldest.

I don't know about you, but I'm beginning to feel like Joan and I are on a fast train to Somewhere. That beats a trip to nowhere! The difference is God, the Lord Jesus, the Holy Spirit, and the host of angels who work day and night keeping us on track.

Approaching the Terminal

Joan and I are terminal. That's right—terminal. And that's okay. The word *terminal* has two basic definitions. It can mean "approaching the end." That's the way doctors employ it with some cancer patients.

It can also mean "a point of connection." The airplane terminal is where you switch flights. An electrical terminal is where power and conduit join forces. A computer terminal is what makes it all happen.

Yes, we are terminal. So are you. We're all heading

for that ultimate point of connection: finite with the infinite, temporal with the eternal, earthly with the heavenly.

In one glorious instant all that we are will be swallowed up in what we are to be. What a moment! No wonder the early Christians prayed, "Come, Lord Jesus!"

Completing the Mission

How can we instill a deep faith in eternal things in our children? How can we open their spiritual eyes to the mystery and adventure that await us as we develop our capacity to see the unseen?

First of all, we must believe these things ourselves—*deeply* believe them in the core of our being. We cannot share what we've been unwilling to commit to our own lives.

Second, we must seize teachable moments to pass these truths to our children. To open their eyes to the wonders in the world around them—the stars, the seasons, the hillsides, the meadows. Then, to open their eyes to God's amazing behind-the-scenes work in their lives.

Hopefully, your teachable moments will not be as traumatic as those in our closing stories. These stories do, however, answer powerfully the question, "Is it important to teach such things to our children?" I think it is.

James Dobson tells the story of the mother of a dying child—a cancer patient at U.C.L.A. Medical Center where Dobson worked. During the last hours of the child's life, a nurse informed the mother that her son was hallucinating. It seems he was, according to the nurse, hearing nonexistent bells ringing.

The mother, however, explained to the nurse that her son was talking about the bells of heaven. You see, as the boy's pain increased, his mom had encouraged him to listen carefully when the pain became absolutely intolerable, and he could hear the bells of heaven ringing. The boy died, cradled in his mother's loving arms, as they listened to the beautiful music of heaven's bells together.

A dad who passed along this same kind of vibrant faith to his young son is in my Sunday school class. Ron Dowdy's story brought tears as it was shared with our class.

> The baseball game was over. It had been a very good game. Yes, we won. My eight-year-old son was an outstanding second baseman for his age. Getting hits at the plate was a little more difficult for him, but his speed and strength continued to improve. I remember his smile when it came his turn to bat and his name was called: **"Steven Dowdy**—next batter." Then his smile slid into that determined look; he felt sure he would get a good hit.

> When we arrived home that summer's day, we were taking in the equipment when Steven said, "Dad, my neck hurts. I feel tired." This was not unusual after a game, but looking at his neck, I saw several large bumps and asked him if a mosquito or something else had bitten him. He wasn't sure. We applied insect bite cream, hoping that would suffice. But the bumps were still there at bedtime and again the following morning.

> The next day at work, I received a call telling me to come to the hospital. I was met in the emergency room by Steven's pediatrician, whom he'd had since he was born, and another doctor I didn't know. Then I saw the rest of the family walking toward us. The news was devastating. I

was told Steven had leukemia. Shock! Horror!
Not my son! There is some mistake! But there
was no mistake.

For months the family tried to live as normally
as we could under that blanket of gloom. Hospi-
tals. Doctors. Clinics. Nurses. Chemotherapy.
One day Steven felt very ill, the next, better.
Then he'd get worse. By the time he returned to
school, he had lost most of his hair due to the
treatments. Our fervent prayer was that he
would get well and be happy. Steven said, "I just
want to be like the other kids again." We just
wanted him to be OK.

One day, Steven told me that someone had asked
him what he had done so bad in his life that God
would make him so sick. In horror, I asked him
what he'd said. "Oh, I just told them they were
mistaken. It was the devil who'd made me sick,
and God would take care of me." Amazed at
Steven's response, I wondered if mine would be
the same.

Steven didn't make it to his ninth birthday. I
remember walking into his hospital room just
hours before he died. Seeing my precious son
lying there, skin and bones, with dark, hollowed
eyes, I could hardly take it. I choked back the
tears and stifled the cry of pain in my chest. Pain
for him and me. Turning away, I looked at the
wall, then up to the ceiling. I couldn't bear to
look at him this way, even for a moment. Then I
heard his soft voice, "Dad, why don't you look at
me?" He must have felt alone. I wondered if God
had felt this way as he saw his Son on the cross.
Could he barely stand it? Did he have to look
away? Again, his voice broke the silence. "Dad, if

you don't take me out of this hospital, I'm going to die." I turned to him, fighting to stay in control of my emotions. "I can't. You have to get well first. But have you forgotten? . . . If you die you'll be with God and Jesus, and that can't be bad after all. You'll get to see all around heaven, and by that time we'll all be together again, even though we'd miss each other badly. I love you very much. What a fine young man you are, and so many people love you." Later that day Steven went to be with Jesus.

At the funeral, people I didn't know, my age, older, and younger, told me they knew Steven. More than one said he had told them stories from the Bible. One couple in their forties said he knocked on their front door one day and told them all about God.

At home again, we were trying to adjust. A vacant chair at the table. An empty bed. Steven was buried on February 20. It was now March. One day my other two children discovered valentine cards with their names on them in their toy box and chest of drawers. There was one left inside the family Bible for me: "To Dad." He had left one for his mommy under her pillow. He knew. God knew.

One evening just before supper, I was trying to catch up with paperwork that had accumulated during the difficult attempt to adapt to Steven's absence. My wife had gone to the grocery store, and the children were playing outside in the yard. Totally absorbed in my activity, I poured over the papers. As I sat there in the kitchen, I heard a voice. "Dad!"

"Yes?" I asked.

"Dad!"

"Yes?" I asked again.

Then I heard, "I'm OK." My mind quickly changed gears, and the hair stood up on the back of my neck. Again, I shouted, "What?" I got the same answer.

"I'm OK."

"Steven!"

Bewildered, yet strangely excited, I ran down the hallway to the bedrooms. There was only one entrance to the hall, and I was next to it. My heart was pounding. I expected to see that little smiling face. Nobody. Confused, I ran back down the hall, through the kitchen, and into the back-yard. I asked my other two children, "Did you call me? Did you shout 'Dad!'?"

"No," they answered. "Are you all right, Daddy?"

I responded, "Yeah, thanks."

Back inside, I just had to check one more time. Slowly, I went back down the hall to Steven's room. I listened. The voice echoed in my head, "Dad, I'm OK." I thought about our prayer, "Father, please make Steven well and happy again. Please don't let him be sick. Please, Father, make him OK." God answered that prayer. Steven is not sick any more. He is well. He is in heaven with God and Jesus. I miss my son, but there's real comfort in knowing where he is.

The faith Ron instilled in Steven gave them both the courage to face one of life's toughest battles—completing the mission of life through death.

And, finally, listen to one dad's letter to his deceased daughter:

My Dear Bristol,

Before you were born I prayed for you. In my heart I knew that you would be a little angel. And so you were.

When you were born on my birthday, April 7, it was evident that you were a special gift from the Lord. But how profound a gift you turned out to be! More than the beautiful bundle of gurgles and rosy cheeks—more than the firstborn of my flesh, a joy unspeakable—you showed me God's love more than anything else in all creation. Bristol, you taught me how to love.

I certainly loved you when you were cuddly and cute, when you rolled over and sat up and jabbered your first words. I loved you when the searing pain of realization took hold that something was wrong—that maybe you were not developing as quickly as your peers, and then when we understood it was more serious than that. I loved you when we went from hospital to clinic to doctor looking for a medical diagnosis that would bring some hope. And, of course, we always prayed for you—and prayed—and prayed. I loved you when one of the tests resulted in too much spinal fluid being drawn from your body and you screamed. I loved you when you moaned and cried, when your mom and I and your sisters would drive for hours late at night to help you fall asleep. I loved you with tears in my eyes when, confused, you would bite your fingers or your lip by accident, and when your eyes crossed and then went blind.

I most certainly loved you when you could no longer speak, and how profoundly I missed your voice! Bristol, I even loved you when you could not say the one thing in life that I longed to hear back—"Daddy, I love you." Bristol, I loved you when I was close to God and when he seemed far away, when I was full of faith and also when I was angry at him.

And the reason I loved you, my Bristol, in spite of these difficulties, is that God put this love in my heart. This is the wondrous nature of God's love, that he loves us even when we are blind, deaf, or twisted—in body or in spirit. God loves us even when we can't tell him that we love him back.

My dear Bristol, now you are free! I look forward to that day, according to God's promises, when we will be joined together with you with the Lord, completely whole and full of joy. I'm so happy that you have your crown first. We will follow you someday—in His time.

Before you were born I prayed for you. In my heart I knew that you would be a little angel. And so you were!

Love, Daddy[1]

Friends in the Fray—Partners in Praise

Helen Keller in her blindness perhaps saw more and better than most of us. She said, "The best and most beautiful things in the world cannot be seen or even touched—they must be felt with the heart."

Angels. Throughout our lives they are our friends in the fray. They protect, encourage, defend, sustain, equip, nurture. They get in the trenches with us. They surround us with power, yet encourage us with warm bread and gentle whispers. They help us complete our mission as they complete theirs.

Angels. For all eternity they will be our partners in praise. We'll join them in what they've been doing since time began: Praising God. What a partnership!

Today, thanks to our angel friends, we walk hand in hand with heaven. Tomorrow, thanks to our Lord Jesus, we'll walk hand in hand in heaven. Together. Forever.

Why should we ever be filled with fear when we are surrounded by such love? **No Fear!** That, my friend, is the calling of angels and the triumphant shout of our heart.

Notes

[1]Reprinted from *When God Doesn't Make Sense* by Dr. James Dobson. © 1993 Tyndale House Publishers. Used by permission. All rights reserved.

Focusing Your Faith:

1. What is the most appealing aspect of heaven to you?

2. Since angels are in and out of heaven, what assignment do you think would be their favorite?

3. What do you believe the role of your personal guardian angel will be when you cross the threshold from this life to the next?

4. How much peace do you have regarding your "terminal" condition? Why?

5. Since we're all terminal, what comfort can we gain from angels to alleviate our fear of dying?

6. What is the key to your being home free? How can angels play a role in it?

7. Pray for God to create within you a joyful expectation for Christ's second coming and our connection with him at last.

Epilogue

It's been many months since he first walked into my counseling office—hollow eyes, icy stares, empty dreams, lonely feelings, deadly thoughts. And scrawled across his chest the words **No Fear**.

I saw him again last week. What a difference! His step, light. His eyes, bright. His smile, wide. Joy and hope exude now from every pore. Fear words don't dominate his vocabulary anymore. Instead, he speaks a lot about love.

Oh, he's certainly had his share of difficulties. His mom is battling cancer. His dad has had a heart attack. And he just discovered last week that he's HIV positive—the result of his years of drug abuse. More than most, he understands that "we're all terminal."

Since he met Jesus, though, he doesn't think or talk much about dying. Instead, he does a lot of living.

He just returned from working with street people in one of America's major cities. He leads a weekly Bible study group at his home church. He's led several people to the Lord.

The change in him would be unbelievable if it weren't so apparent. His words from last week still echo in my ear: "I think it's time we stopped being afraid to celebrate the dynamic activity of God in our lives."

I think he's right.

As he turned to leave, I noticed scrawled across the back of his T-shirt the words **He Is Risen**.

I thought to myself: Jesus really does make all

the difference in the world, doesn't he? No wonder angels point all eyes toward him. Have you, friend, given Jesus a chance to make all the difference within you?

Please . . .

Please . . . !

Whatever you do . . .

Don't be afraid to give Jesus a chance.

No Fear!

Additional Faith*Focus* Book Titles:

The Power Zone
Jesus' Model for a New Humanity
by Larry Calvin

Loosening Your Grip
Letting Go and Living in True Security
by Harold Shank

In the Name of Jesus
Receiving Power from the Prayers of
the New Testament by Gary Holloway

The Most Excellent Way
Overcoming Chronic Issues That
Divide the Church by Eldred Echols

One Holy Hunger
Discovering the God You've Never
Known by Mike Cope

Sinai Summit
Meeting God with Our Character Crisis
by Rick Atchley

**Haven't You Heard? There's a WAR
Going On!**
Unlocking the Code to Revelation
by Eldred Echols

Discovering the Pearl of Great Price
The Parables of Jesus
by Eldred Echols

Call 1-800-531-5220 and ask about the
Faith*Focus* **Individual Membership Program**
to complete your own faith-building library.